HOMES *with* HEART

HOMES *with* HEART

Turning Living Spaces into Loving Places

RUTH FROST, M.DIV

Copyright © 2021, Ruth Frost, M.Div

All rights reserved. No part of this publication may be reproduced, distributed, or transmitted in any form or by any means, including photocopying, recording, digital scanning, or other electronic or mechanical methods, without the prior written permission of the publisher, except in the case of brief quotations embodied in critical reviews and certain other noncommercial uses permitted by copyright law. For permission requests, please address She Writes Press.

Published 2021
Printed in the United States of America
Print ISBN: 978-1-64742-118-2
E-ISBN: 978-1-64742-119-9
Library of Congress Control Number: 2020924584

Book design by Stacey Aaronson

For information, address:
She Writes Press
1569 Solano Ave #546
Berkeley, CA 94707

She Writes Press is a division of SparkPoint Studio, LLC.

Names and identifying characteristics have been changed to protect the privacy of certain individuals.

This book is dedicated with deep gratitude to my families:
my first family, my current family, and our families of the heart.

It is also dedicated to the families of the world:
those who struggle to make home here,
and to all who leave this world a better place.

Contents

Poem: Where Is Home? | 1
Preface: The Search for Home | 3

PART ONE

COMING HOME TO OURSELVES

1: Welcome, Refuge, and Belonging | 9
2: Coming Home to Myself | 15
3: Creating Home Together | 23
4: Leaving Home to Follow a Dream | 27

PART TWO

FINDING HOME WITHIN COMMUNITY

5: Celebration and Prosecution | 33
6: Hospitality in the Era of AIDS | 41
7: Getting to Know Our Homeless Neighbors | 47
8: Family Ties within Community | 53
9: Two Moms, Two Dads, and One Baby | 59
10: Embracing Transitions Together | 67
11: Wedding Bells and Other Miracles | 71

PART THREE

MAKING LIVING SPACES LOVING PLACES

12: Homing with Children | 81

13: Mapping and Blessing Our Homes | 91

14: The Power of Ritual in Homing | 97

15: Honoring a Home Legacy | 107

16: Healing Painful Associations with Home | 115

17: Overcoming Clutter with Sacred Giving | 121

18: Using Symbols to Hold Memories | 129

19: Homes Occupied by Work and Electronics | 133

20: Creating Decor That Tells Your Story | 139

PART FOUR

FORMING AND SUPPORTING FAMILIES

21: Choosing Families of the Heart | 147

22: Becoming Family | 153

23: Animal Companions as Family | 161

24: Protecting Intimacy in Partnerships | 165

25: Crossing Life Thresholds | 171

26: Tipping Points for Change | 179

27: Families Seeking Refuge | 185

28: Opening Home and Heart | 191

PART FIVE

GOING HOME: STORIES FROM HOSPICE

29: Held in Blessing from Birth to Death | 203

30: Lessons in Living from the Dying | 209

31: Meeting Heart to Heart When Memory Fades | 217

32: Cultivating a Vibrant Spiritual Life | 223

33: Marked by Love | 231

34: Brian's Journey Home | 235

35: Homeless to Homecoming | 239

Afterword | 245

Notes | 247

Acknowledgments | 253

About the Author | 255

Reading Group Guide | 257

Where Is Home?

Home is where someone is expecting you,
where eyes shine their greeting
as you cross the threshold,
and a bark trumpets you to the household.

Home is where you
lay down whatever is burdening you,
tell whatever is bothering you,
and let yourself be found.

Home is where a memory, a dream,
a laugh, or a tear is freely shared,
until "my" story becomes "our" story
and endings become beginnings.

Home is where welcoming arms await you
as you come into this world,
and sending hands bless you
when you leave it.

Home is the company you keep until departure time,
watching with you through the night
until the rising sun lights your way.

Family is all your loved ones in whom you "home"
here and hereafter.
Love is the way home.

~ *Ruth Frost, a poem inspired by my father*

Preface

THE SEARCH FOR HOME

Homes with Heart is written for everyone who wants to take the next step in home living, which is home life design. We have all heard the saying "Home is where your heart is." But when our hearts are weary or wounded or our lives uprooted, it's hard to find home. Sometimes we struggle to be at home within ourselves or at home with one another. This book encompasses our journey to find and make home in the world. It provides guidance in turning living spaces into loving places that become "homes with heart." Together, we explore how to create the homes we want to live in, how we choose families to enrich our living, and how caring communities can expand our experience of home. Ideally, our homes should express who we are and support the quality of life we seek, in the company of those we love.

As we search for home within ourselves and create home around us, we will look at some of the obstacles that can interfere with making "homes with heart" and explore ways to overcome them. We will also consider how we can redefine family more generously to include "families of choice," or "families of the heart," as I prefer to name them. Whether we live singly, with friends, or in family groups, the people in our lives shape and are shaped by the kind of homes we nurture. Over time, the homes we create will embody our stories and invite new stories from those who cross their threshold.

In writing this book, I relate some experiences in my life and my partner's life that have had a formative influence on how we "home" together. I share how one special community extended extraordinary hospitality to us, and how we have drawn upon family of the heart to enrich our home life wherever we have lived. Included in this writing are conversations I have had with other people to further our understanding of the various ways people create home and family. All of this has strengthened my conviction that creating home is a relational and spiritual adventure that transcends mere habitation of physical space. We discover meaning and purpose when our living spaces become loving places.

When we work to turn our living spaces into loving places with the help of supportive communities, caring friends, and families of the heart, our homes sing. At their best, our homes have the power to both shelter us and renew us for the good work we do in the world. How we live in our homes will guide who we are in the world. When we extend refuge to those in search of safety, welcome, and belonging, we become part of the world's family.

After twenty-seven years together, my partner and I fulfilled a late-in-life dream by purchasing our first (and likely last) home in an older historic urban neighborhood that was known for its preservation of bungalows built in the first three decades of the twentieth century. Five years later, we were invited to show our home in the Twin Cities Craftsman Bungalow Home Tour of Minneapolis/St. Paul. The day of the tour, we were amazed and delighted to host over five hundred guests in our small home.

Six months later, our family expanded to include our first grandbaby and his parents, who now live with us, together with our dog and cat. Baby paraphernalia has invaded our space. What was a showcase house for the tour has become a thoroughly lived-in home. Spit-up rags are draped over the arm of every chair, a playpen hides underneath the dining room table, and pet toys mingled with baby toys are strewn about everywhere. The house still has great ambience but much less order—and a lot more heart!

My hope is that these reflections inspire you to strengthen the heart of your home so you may find refuge within it, create your own family of the heart to enrich the joy of sharing it, and overcome those obstacles to "homing" that inhibit your freedom to fully live in it. If this book can help you accomplish this, it will have fulfilled its purpose, and you will have created a home with heart.

When we live with intention, we can be at home wherever we are. As we walk this journey together, may we all turn our living spaces into loving places that become "homes with heart." In doing so, we embrace the dream of the world that extends hospitality to everyone. We discover friendship among strangers. In the words of Ram Dass, "All we are doing is walking each other home." [1] What if that is the most important thing we do in this life?

As a retired hospice chaplain, I have been deeply privileged to learn from many people with diverse spiritual perspectives and traditions as they prepared to go home and made their passage. What I have witnessed at their bedsides has convinced me that our life in this world is but one segment of our journey to carry home within us and create home around us. I have concluded my reflections with a few stories from my work in hospice. I have come to believe that ultimately, finding home means taking a spiritual journey in good company. We are all one. Together, the way home is love.

Note: All content in this book is based on actual events and actual people, but some names, places, and details have been altered or withheld for the purpose of protecting individuals' privacy. Interviews are used by permission of the interviewees with their privacy similarly protected as desired.

Coming Home to Ourselves

It was a crowded department store at holiday time. Harried people milled about, vying for the sale items. Waiting for my friend to finish her shopping, I noticed a small child in distress. He was alone, having been lured away by the toy aisle and now realizing he had become separated from his mother. As he called out for her through tears, I approached to comfort him. He looked at me, wanting to come to me—to anyone who could help—but knowing he was not supposed to speak to strangers, he stood frozen in panic and then backed away, still crying. I stopped my approach and asked a store clerk to announce where he was while I kept an eye on him just far away enough not to cause him to bolt.

The announcement of a lost child echoed over the loudspeaker with directions as to his whereabouts. Soon his mother arrived. He ran to her and threw both arms around her leg. As he looked up at her, she bent over, shaking her finger in his tear-stained face, and screamed, "How many times have I told you not to wander off? When we get home you'll get what you deserve!" My heart sank, wondering what home was like for him. I don't know their story and cannot judge their circumstances. But I ached for the little one who was lost and then found, but not welcomed home.

His need haunted me that day, and I wonder how he is, forty-five years later. His need is everyone's need—to be found when we are lost, to be enfolded in the arms of love, and to be welcomed home."

~ Ruth Frost, *Journal Memories*

Welcome, Refuge, and Belonging

Remember the greeting of hospitality people offered when they were happy to welcome you into their home? "Come in, make yourself at home!" If you were staying awhile, the greeting might be followed by "Our home is your home." You might respond by taking your shoes off before crossing the threshold out of respect for the homeowner's welcome. In some cultures, you might even receive a footbath for soothing tired, sore feet.

These greetings of welcome speak to the truth that a home isn't complete until it moves from being a solitary sanctuary to a place of communal care. It also suggests that the longing for home is a universal longing for welcome, safety, and inclusion. Home is fundamentally a state of belonging, whether we make ourselves "at" home or make ourselves "a" home. Home is intended to nurture life and relationships formed in the course of life. A couple of centuries ago, "home" was where we were born, where we grew up, and where we died. Today, in our highly mobile society, a house is often regarded chiefly as a financial asset—a hedge against an insecure future. But when homes held the sum of our days, they became sacred vessels for life and love.

At the conclusion of an interview with James Lipton, host of *Inside the Actors Studio*, actress Meryl Streep was asked the usual question posed to all interviewees who appeared on the show. The show was taped with a live audience of student actors, directors, and teachers. The question was, "If heaven is real, what would you most like to hear God say when you stand before the pearly gates?" Without a moment's hesitation, Streep, with a radiant smile, called out, "*Every*body in!" Ultimately, that is home: a sanctuary in which everyone can experience complete belonging, universal welcome, and unconditional love. It is a realm of light, of peace and healing.

That is, of course, the ideal. Many of us fall far short of receiving and offering that ideal. Some children are not born into the welcoming arms of love but are born into the empty hands of want. Others do not know physical shelter. Many live in households where safety and well-being have been co-opted by addiction or domestic abuse or mental illness; others are living in countries engaged in armed conflict. Some are in a state of exile, refugees far from home. Many do not know what home could or should be.

Whether it is family neglect or abuse, the violence of war, or cultural marginalization due to class, racism, poverty, or gender identity, the human race has not provided home for all its members. Those of us who come from economic privilege and have been raised in households that have been able to provide both security and love are obligated to pay attention to the needs of the world's children who live in more perilous circumstances. We are all one human family, learning to create homes founded in hospitality and families grounded in love.

I once heard an interviewer ask virtuoso violinist Anne-Sophie Mutter what a performer needed to do in order to be ready for a concert performance. She replied, "Assuming you have already practiced, you must first understand the soul of the music, and then you must sing to the heart of your audience." [2]

I wonder if a similar process takes place in the transformation of a house into a home. We may be custodians of a house where others have lived before us or will live after us. But how we live in our house will determine if it ever becomes a home for ourselves as well as a welcoming experience for those who cross its threshold. If it does, our home will change with us and work its own changes upon us. We can make music in our homes if we understand their soulful purpose. Guests will participate in the music making if our home has a heart that connects with the hearts of others.

I believe the heart of every house is its hearth. By hearth, I mean whatever draws family and friends together, whether a literal fireplace hearth, the warmth of a kitchen when our favorite foods are being prepared, or the table around which we eat and tell stories, play games, and sometimes work out family issues. The hearth is a gathering space that draws us into community. But it can also hold our private moments that comfort and sustain us. In the late-night hours we may read ourselves into far-flung worlds that stretch our beliefs and inspire our imaginations. In the quiet, early-morning hours before no one else has risen but the birds, we may sit eavesdropping on the sounds of creation and marvel at our place in it or contemplate a difficult problem and draw hope from a new dawn.

As a child, I was fortunate to grow up in a large home built in 1905 that our family did not own but that came as part of the benefit of my father's job. He was a seminary professor at a time when professors' salaries were very modest, but the house our family of six got to enjoy as part of his employment benefit was a gift to our family life that lasted until his retirement, when his children were grown and busy with our own lives. It became a beloved family home in our twenty years living there.

These are a few of my favorite childhood memories from that home:

discovering a treasure trove of Nancy Drew mysteries on one rainy day's exploration of the gabled attic; lying in the dark imagining myself held high up in the five old oak trees whose gnarled branches cradled our house and tapped at my window; waking up to the smell of coffee and my mother's fresh baked bread on a Saturday morning; watching my oldest sister, Miriam, meticulously paint angels on our front window during the holidays; rising early Christmas Day to enjoy the soft glow of the tree in the company of my other sister, Naomi, careful to heed her admonition: "Don't talk—it destroys the magic"; making card table "bear dens" in the basement with my younger brother, John, and playing the bear in my mother's moth-eaten fur coat; lying on the rug by the fire, listening to my father tell stories from his youth on the family farm until I could recite the names of all their horses; and, finally, reading underneath my mother's baby grand piano so I could watch the play of emotions flit across her expressive face as she let music take her somewhere beyond us. Those are some of the memories that enriched and shaped me in that home.

Of course there were other kinds of memories too: of difficult lessons learned, secrets hidden away, losses endured, and sharp words heatedly exchanged with the same people we love. These also find their way into our homes and put their stamp upon us. Our homes contain both the wonder and the messes of our lives. Their rooms are the silent witnesses to who we are becoming within them and what memories we will carry when we leave them. They reflect our joys and sorrows, our fears and failures, and our hopes and dreams.

Our homes are the libraries of our lives, whose rooms preserve our stories—those that sustain us, and those that still haunt us. Our stories are our reference points, but as with all reference books, they invite course correction as new knowledge and new experience enlightens, and sometimes supplants, the old. The present, lived with compassionate wisdom, illumines the past and lends hope to the future.

Recently, I had an opportunity to go to an exhibit at our local art institute that featured the struggles of the world's refugees who have been disenfranchised from home. Attached to the wall of one exhibit there were anonymous notes scrawled in pencil, written in response to the question: "What is home?" Three of them stopped me in my tracks. The first read, "Home is a time when people are there for each other, where people can grow unthreatened." The second said, "Home is a place in your heart where there is no judgment, where your heart sings and you can breathe." The third said simply, "Home is what was taken from me." As we "home" in this world, we must never forget that "justice is what love looks like in public." [3] We start where it begins, in our own home with our own families. We start with ourselves.

2

Coming Home to Myself

For a very long time, I struggled to come to terms with a secret I had carried from early childhood well into adulthood. My secret was that my identity didn't match the cultural norm of my generation. I am lesbian, a term that was not commonly in use back in the day I needed to know it and claim it. My secret was compounded by the fact that I was led to believe that claiming my lesbian identity would put me in an eternal state of conflict with my Christian heritage and imperil my soul. What actually imperiled my soul was internalized homophobia because of the negative messages from both church and society, neither of which understood that this was a matter of identity that needed to be fully integrated, not renounced. My situation was complicated by the fact that I felt called to ministry at a time when most Christian denominations prohibited gay and lesbian people from serving as ordained ministers. Ministry became a dream deferred.

When I think of my life in terms of a play in three acts, it is easy to see how each act represents distinctly different life stages. In a typical play, the first act commonly functions to set the stage and introduce the principal characters, the second act develops the story, and the third act makes sense of the first two, integrating them and revealing the meaning of the whole. I spent the first act of my life living in the shadows of the closet, my "life play" stalled with respect to authentic character development. The cracks of light that managed to penetrate my darkness came from those "out" lesbian pioneers who blazed the way before me, allowing me to follow their trail at a distance until I could discover and claim my own path. The early feminist movement of the seventies scared me and sustained me at the same time. I wasn't yet ready for it, but it gave me hope and a glimpse into another world, both dangerous and free.

During the first act of my life play, I seesawed between denying my sexuality and accepting my sexuality. However, I saw no way to openly embrace my sexuality without abandoning my religious roots, a step I was not prepared to take. This eventually led to a misbegotten marriage to a gay man that was naively intended to help both of us "adapt" to heterosexuality, but which instead devolved into a profoundly unhappy situation in which body, soul, and heart were perpetually conflicted. Turning to our pastor for guidance, we entered counseling aimed at shoring up our questionable union. When this proved utterly ineffective, my husband became dangerously depressed. It was time to end an untenable situation before it led to irrevocable harm. We parted company sadly but with the weight of an impossible union lifted.

With no safety to embrace my lesbian identity in the light of freedom and openness, it took me several years to get to a place of deep peace and bold self-acceptance that could then truly yield life-affirming relationships. I made serious mistakes in those closeted years that were deeply hurtful to people I loved before I could finally and fully realize self-acceptance and well-being in relationships.

In 1980, still closeted, I resumed trying to pursue my dream of parish ministry and entered seminary. Toward the completion of the four-year masters of divinity degree, I had an interview with my candidacy committee and was approved for ordination. I then went on to interview with a bishop of the district to which I was assigned that was a large metro area. The interview went well because when asked why my husband and I had divorced, I spoke only half the truth: that we had divorced because my husband was gay. The bishop's response was to say that I would be a valuable asset to his district as there had been several gay male pastors who had "come out" while in ministry before resigning their positions. He stated, "None of these pastors had been open with me when they first accepted calls, so I couldn't go to bat for them. It's been a mess for their congregations." When I asked if a qualified gay applicant who had been fully open with him from the start would be eligible to receive a call, he replied sharply, "No, and that will never happen!" He then added, "You would be a good resource for the wives of these men." The interview ended with a warm welcome to the area and his assurance that he had a parish in mind for me, adding that I would be hearing from him in a month.

I left this interview feeling absolutely crazy and thinking, *What shall I do?* Exiting the office building, I stepped out onto the city sidewalk just as the gay pride parade was passing. I stood there frozen, a deer in the headlights, looking at hundreds of gay people bearing down on me waving signs that read, "I'm gay and I'm proud!" Their energy was electric, a juggernaut of pride and joy. I thought to myself, *I can't say I'm gay in this church, and I certainly can't say I'm proud.* It was a pivotal moment. I returned to Minnesota and then contacted the district office, "postponing" the call process for a year to give myself space to think. I used the year to intern in the field of chemical dependency treatment services. At the end of the year, I let my candidacy status expire.

Borrowed light is better than no light, and there was just enough of it to reveal the mess that was my life in the closet. I finally grasped that love cannot survive a closeted existence or become truly life-giving if secreted. It can only become an incomplete version of itself—distorted by fear and shame, internalized from heterosexism and homophobia. Good therapy, self-forgiveness, and the loving support of my family and friends have accompanied me on my path to wholeness. Giving up the dream of ministry in order to fully claim an authentic life became a fundamental prerequisite to freedom.

I was nearly thirty-seven by the time my personal development was fully integrated. Committing to living my life openly allowed my second act to belatedly emerge. I was at last ready to "come out of the closet" to my then older parents, having been graced with the love of a woman with whom I hoped to share the rest of my life uncloseted. It had also dawned on me that my fear of losing my parents if I came out to them was already being realized. In protecting myself from being truly known, I had erected a guard around my emotional life that kept them increasingly at a distance. I was in danger of becoming lost to them. Fortunately, by that time I was "out" to my siblings, who were all supportive. It was time to gather my courage and bridge the remaining divide. I called my sister Naomi and asked her to be present, knowing I could count on her to support both my parents and me.

On that fateful autumn evening, I decided to drop by my brother's house briefly for moral support before going on to my parents' home near his. John met me at the door and refused to let me in. Instead he said, "Get your butt over to Mom and Dad's! Naomi has been waiting for you all evening. Mom keeps making her sing opera arias, and she's had it. No more stalling!" I obeyed my marching orders.

I could hear my sister's soprano and my mother's piano accompaniment as I walked up the front steps to the house. As I entered, Mother cheerily invited me to take a chair by the piano saying, "Listen to this, Ruthie." Naomi shot me a look that told me I had better stop the musical portion of the evening and get on with business. When I said, "No, I have something I need to talk to you about first," both Mom and Dad snapped to immediate attention as all of us sat down.

I had a carefully rehearsed speech, honed over many years and revised as many times. I got about two sentences into my speech. They were, "Mom, Dad, I have something to tell you. It has taken me a long time to come to terms with myself, but I need you to know that I am homosexual" (fearing they wouldn't know what "lesbian" meant). Before I could go any further, my father sprang from his chair, dropping to his knees in front of my chair. Placing his hands on my shoulders, he met my eyes with his steady gaze and said, "My, how much you must have suffered keeping yourself a secret from us all these years. I hope you know we love you and nothing can ever change that." Then he kissed me on my forehead and gathered me into his arms. Over his shoulder, I could see my mother, wide-eyed, nodding in vigorous agreement with my father's declaration of unconditional love and my sister smiling in relief. It was a stunning response to my disclosure that far exceeded my expectations.

We talked long and fully that evening, and I shared my hope that my relationship with Phyllis would be a lasting one as close as theirs. I told them I was sick of hiding myself and could not hide Phyllis or the joy she brought to my life. I was done with living a clandestine life. I wanted a life of authenticity and purpose, and to achieve this, I knew I needed to live my own life openly as a lesbian, even if it meant letting go of ministry. It was clear that Dad was more at ease with our conversation than Mom, but she was no less determined to be supportive. At some point in the evening, my mother declared, "Well! I think it's time for some ice cream!" That was the day I fully came home to myself. It was a powerful homecoming, liberating for all of us and capped with celebration. For my father and me, it afforded us two precious years of knowing and being fully known. My second act had finally begun.

In 1986, we chose to affirm our commitment in the presence of friends, family, and the local chapter of Lutherans Concerned, a sanctuary movement for lesbian, gay, and bisexual people within the national church. In our simple ceremony, we exchanged vows before all those in attendance, which miraculously included all the members of both our families. Naomi sang Samuel Barber's "Sure on This Shining Night" with my mother accompanying her on the piano. Friends offered readings and their own words of blessing, as did Phyllis's brother and my brother. At the reception afterward, Phyllis's mother talked to a seminary professor who attended our celebration and wondered aloud what kind of future we would have together in this society. He replied wisely, "The uncertainty of that is all the more reason why we need to support them in their life together."

By the time of our commitment ceremony, both of us had received our masters of divinity degrees. However, each of us had let go of our dreams of ministry in order to claim freedom to love one another openly. By then, Phyllis had become another daughter to both my parents and "sister out-of-law" (as they liked to teasingly call her) to my siblings. I found work at Pride Institute, a pioneering program for gay, lesbian, bisexual, and transgender people seeking treatment for chemical dependency. There, the reality and concerns of LGBT lives could be supported and normed. There, I could have Phyllis's picture on my desk. It was a simple yet profound change. For me, our openly celebrated love dissolved years of internalized heterosexism and homophobia.

Working at Pride Institute completed the "coming out" process I had tentatively begun through Lutherans Concerned. Pride utilized the Twelve Steps of AA as well as some other approaches to sobriety. In addition to meaningful work, Pride offered me a venue for spiritual growth and expression without the homophobic strictures of parish ministry. Recognizing my gifts and training, this secular, for-profit institution utilized me as a spiritual counselor while hiring me for the official position of continuing care coordinator. We were all aware that the false choice between spirituality and sexuality imposed on so many gay people heightened the probability of relapse in sobriety. In addition to coordinating post-treatment care for clients, I was asked to hear Fifth Steps and to facilitate groups for people in recovery who were struggling to integrate spirituality with sexuality. This proved helpful to many.

Meanwhile, Phyllis, having given up her own dream of ministry but still uncertain as to what direction to go in her professional life, volunteered as a group facilitator with children and families affected by HIV/AIDS. Our work was outside the church but no less important to either of us. At the time, we couldn't have foreseen that it would both prepare us for, and eventually lead us back to, an opportunity for specialized ministry.

Just a year after our commitment ceremony, my father was diagnosed with terminal cancer and died that spring. The week after his diagnosis, he made a point of connecting with each of his adult children and with his beloved granddaughter, Rachel, to share his heart with us. In what was to be our last visit with him, Phyllis and I sat on either side of his recliner, each of us holding one of his hands. Turning to Phyllis, he said, "I never thought I could love someone so much to whom I was not related by blood. You have been another daughter to me." And to both of us he continued, "I am sorry you have each had to give up your dreams of ministry in order to claim yourselves and your life together. The world and the church can be so cruel in their ignorance. But I don't fear for you as a couple. Your problems will not be internal but external. And wherever you are, you will always be doing ministry, because ministry is *who* you are." And with those words of blessing, he set our spiritual compass.

Realizing we would not have another opportunity, I chose to tell my father that Phyllis and I had decided we would have a child together through artificial insemination with what at that time we thought would be an anonymous donor. I finished by saying, "I'm not sure when it will happen, but we know it *will* happen. When it does, I want to know that I had told you." He responded by squeezing our hands and saying, "I have no frame of reference for this new thing you will be doing. But I trust you." In the short time remaining, Dad used up his waning strength receiving visits from many former students and colleagues who wanted to say goodbye to him.

In his last days with us, our family gathered at his bedside for Holy Communion. I asked his visiting pastor to use the communion set which had belonged to Dad's father, who had also been a parish pastor. My grandfather always had it with him when he called on people who were ill at home. That communion set showed all the signs of heavy use, having traveled more miles by horse and buggy than it had by car. When we had communion at Dad's bedside, he was no longer able to swallow, so we just touched the elements to his lips. He responded to the Prayer of Jesus by opening his eyes and folding his hands. My father's last words to my mother before he became too weak to speak were, "Thank you for letting me die. Forgive everything. Remember the best." After Dad's death, my mother gave me my grandfather's communion set. I cherish it as a talisman of an intergenerational spiritual legacy passed on to a granddaughter my grandfather had never known.

I am so glad that I was able to claim myself before it would have been too late to share my life fully with my father. His body was laid to rest under a beautiful white pine in a small woodland cemetery. The headstone has carved into it these words: *The dream is ended. This is the morning.* [4] They reflect my father's trust that from the vantage point of this life, the best is yet to come.

3

Creating Home Together

In our first five years together in Minneapolis, Phyllis and I lived in a tiny efficiency apartment in the bottom-level family room of a private home. It was a "home within a home" shared with Jean, our elderly landlady. Since Phyllis had originally rented the space as a single person, we needed to let Jean know we had become a couple and wished to live together. Bracing herself for a possible adverse reaction, Phyllis nervously approached Jean. Noticing her trepidation, Jean asked, "What's wrong? Is there something you don't like about the apartment? Something you want me to change?" Phyllis then said that she and I had become "more than friends" and would like to live together as a couple. Jean replied, "Is that all? I suspected as much. I grew up in Berkeley, you know. Don't worry, I will afford you the same privacy I would afford a married couple." During the five years we lived there, Jean was as good as her word.

We started out with very little in the way of furnishings for our new home. This gave us an opportunity to be quite intentional about how we filled that small space. From the outset of our relationship, Phyllis was candid about the fact that she had grown up in a family home that reflected her parents' financial struggles, their reluctance to buy anything new, and their unwillingness to replace or part with anything even when beyond repair. Her family home would be described today as that of hoarders, complicated by the chaos of an alcoholic family system.

"Order is a therapeutic issue for me, Ruth," she said. "I so want it, but I haven't yet learned how to create it. I never invited friends into our family home because I was ashamed of it. I knew it wasn't like their homes. There was just too much stuff and too much ongoing chaos to keep anything clean. Even though I tried, I couldn't fix it. I'm afraid to buy or collect much of anything now because I worry I'll fall into the trap I grew up in." Having long been fascinated by space design and how organization and creativity both play a role in developing a personal home aesthetic, I was happy to take responsibility for order. Phyllis took on much of the cleaning and derived great satisfaction from being able to clean in an environment that was relatively uncluttered and well organized. We made a good team.

Together, we determined what we needed and where each item would "live" in our small open floor plan. This meant practicing a good deal of selectivity without sacrificing beauty to necessity. A common mantra of ours became, "Order reveals beauty and supports hospitality." No matter how beautiful one's possessions, they cannot be seen or well used if they are embedded in clutter. Or, as a gay male friend was fond of saying, "Remember, too much wonderful is still too much." We knew that becoming trapped in clutter buries beauty and chokes hospitality. We made a serious commitment to both order and hospitality, with the added value of comfort so guests would quickly feel at home.

My skills as a stained glass designer and Phyllis's talent as a musician meant that I needed space to do my commission work of windows and lamps, and Phyllis needed space for a piano in order to play and compose. We managed to accomplish both. When I needed to do a commission, I simply covered a double sink in the laundry area with plywood as my work surface. We purchased a compact studio piano that perfectly fit the remaining wall space next to the closet. For the living room area, we needed only a love seat and a rocker, augmented with some plush accent pillows on a thick rug by the fireplace for additional seating when entertaining small gatherings.

We successfully scrounged secondhand stores and garage sales for hidden treasures. Two such items we picked up for our small space were a dresser painted hot orange, which we refinished to reveal its beautiful oak grain, and a dining room table with leaves that gave it the capacity to seat up to ten people. The dresser we stuck in our closet because we had no room for it elsewhere, and the table we kept small, storing the extra leaves for future use. Our stained glass lamps and well-used fireplace provided us with plenty of soft lighting and cozy ambience. Our friends were amazed by the transformation of that small space and its charm. Some even teasingly suggested we offer it as a weekend bed and breakfast in exchange for a stay in their more spacious homes. Unwittingly, we had anticipated the tiny house movement of today and delighted in it.

This home arrangement developed into a mutually caring household with a weekly evening devoted to furthering our bond with Jean over a PBS mystery series or conversations about a good book with a bowl of popcorn or a glass of sherry. We all looked forward to these ritualized evenings together. A retired librarian, Jean loved to discuss what she was reading with other serious readers. She poignantly confided that since her husband's death a few years earlier, she had mounded books on his side of their bed so their weight would feel like his, and their contents would provide the comfort of late-night company. As time passed, we discovered that in creating our first home with Jean, we also formed our first experience of "family of the heart," though we didn't name it as such at the time.

We enjoyed our "home within a home" together with Jean for five years. When it was time to move, she declared she would not rent to anyone else because she didn't think she could ever match the family experience we had created together. We were grateful she lived long enough to rejoice with us in the birth of our baby daughter three years later. Jean died a short while after. This experience in forming family of the heart with Jean has been repeated in various locales over the course of our thirty-four years together. Each left their stamp upon us, particularly as we became intentional in naming who we were to one another.

Leaving Home to Follow a Dream

In late 1989, each of us having given up the dream of parish ministry, our dreams were returned to us beyond expectation or measure. Phyllis and I received unusual calls to ministry in San Francisco. Two congregations, St. Francis Lutheran and First United Lutheran, together with a coalition of Bay Area Lutheran clergy and congregational leaders, independently issued calls to us and to our colleague Jeff Johnson. We would each be doing pastoral ministry in our respective churches—Jeff at First United, and Phyllis and I at St. Francis. However, we were also charged with developing an outreach ministry that was to provide support, spiritual care, and advocacy with and on behalf of lesbian, gay, and bisexual people as well as people with HIV/AIDS. As time passed and awareness grew, our advocacy would extend to transgender people as well. The scope of our work included challenging national church attitudes and policies restricting the full participation, recognition, and support of these populations in the wider church. It was to become a national ministry working in alliance with other like-minded ministries. This was a daunting prospect and an equally amazing opportunity—one that was to depend on a great many people across the country partnering with us in this work.

Shortly before our move to San Francisco, one of the professors at the seminary we had attended in St. Paul invited me to speak to his class about this new ministry opportunity. After accepting his invitation, which was open to others who might wish to come as well, I was immediately contacted by the dean and told I needed to meet with the president of the seminary. She said he wanted to know what I planned to talk about. Suspecting this did not bode well, I nevertheless agreed to the meeting.

During our meeting, the president asked me why I wished to address the class. I responded by speaking to the importance of this ministry to those populations marginalized by church and society and suffering under the twin burdens of prejudice and rejection. I expressed hope that my remarks could answer some questions and concerns within the community and build bridges of understanding between straight people and lesbian and gay people of faith. I then added that, as the daughter of a highly regarded former professor at the seminary, and as one who had grown up on its campus since early childhood, the seminary had been my home, and many in the community had known me from childhood into adulthood. The president replied flatly, "Well, now that you are a public figure, the rules have changed, and the child can never come home." With that, our interview was over and the invitation to speak on campus withdrawn. When word of this got around the following day, the courageous professor re-invited me to speak in his home off campus. The standing-room-only crowd that evening couldn't have been more hospitable.

On a return trip to visit my mother, who was living in her own small home a block away from the big house I grew up in, I mentioned to her that I wished I could show Phyllis the old house. My mother assured me that the seminary professor and his wife living there were good friends of hers and would gladly give me the opportunity to relive with Phyllis some of the memories it held. Busy with the many obligations we tried to pack into this short trip, we ran out of time.

It wasn't until the following year, when we were again in Minnesota to see my mother, that I impulsively decided to stop at the old house first to inquire if I could show Phyllis the ground floor living space. A woman I did not recognize answered the door. I introduced both of us and made my inquiry. "I know perfectly well who you are, and I despise you and everything you stand for!" was her swift retort. Taken aback, I paused, speechless. Then she went on, "But having said that, you may come in." What followed was an uncomfortable, surreal tour of the downstairs. But determined to honor the memories important to me, I shared a few vignettes with Phyllis as we toured, the current occupant in silent accompaniment. Afterward, as she ushered us to the front door, the homeowner said, "I, too, grew up in an old house that our family loved. If I could have revisited it, I would have wanted to receive the same hospitality I extended to you." We thanked her and made a hasty exit, shaking our heads in disbelief.

In conversation with my mother later that day, I learned that her friends had moved, and I had met the new resident. This strange experience left a sad association with a beloved home, but I realized that the true homecoming had taken place long ago. I had come home to myself.

Twenty-five years later, my mother long since deceased, I was to have a second opportunity to revisit the old house. By that time, it had ceased being a family residence and had become home to a yoga center. I learned from my brother that the old house was to be demolished to make way for a senior living complex. Before it vacated, the center invited the community to an open house in celebration of solstice.

That evening, Phyllis and I once again approached the old house. This time the front walkway was lined with glowing ice luminaries casting candlelight on a peace labyrinth marked out in the snow alongside it.

The front porch had been festooned with pine boughs. An aroma of hot cider mingled with pine issued from the open door. We spent the evening in the company of a lovely group of yogic meditators and neighborhood residents celebrating solstice together. It was the end of an era for a remarkable home, beloved by many and culminating in a peaceful goodbye for me, filled with gratitude and the gift of light.

A few months later, the demolition of the old house was completed. My brother bought its beautiful front door from the salvage company that had stripped the house of all its mahogany woodwork. I like to think of the wood of that house living on in the homes of many other people, like scattered ashes of a loved one that become part of the ongoing cycle of death and new life. I am glad that the door has remained with our family, an abiding symbol of hospitality within community.

Finding Home Within Community

We all long to find our tribe. But easy affinity will not feed our inner hunger to make our lives count, to make our struggles worth the pain. The quest for community will redefine our humanity when we meld the 'common' (our shared public life) with a fuller 'unity' (commitment to harmony). 'Common-unity' strives for justice within diversity. Creating community means we are humble enough to listen and confident enough to let the light of love lead us. Together we make the world a better home, whether we reach across borders or across neighborhoods. Community has no *other*—only *us together.*"

~ Phyllis Zillhart,
from a workshop on "Strengthening Communal Ties"

Celebration and Prosecution

In 1990, three weeks after our arrival in San Francisco, we were honored to experience the joy of being ordained in a joint service with our colleague Jeff Johnson. The Evangelical Lutheran Church in America (ELCA) had declared the ordinations "irregular" and "out of order." However, they were affirmed as "extraordinary" in a letter of support from Krister Stendahl, respected religious leader with the World Council of Churches. Stendahl saw the Church not as a monument to the past but as a river of life-giving water in ever-changing times. His joyful recasting of our ordinations as "extraordinary" was embraced by all who participated in them. In addition to the thousand who attended the service in San Francisco, another thousand gathered at seven other sites around the country that were connected to ours via satellite. News coverage was extensive both at home and abroad. This resulted in voluminous amounts of mail—most of it supportive. It revealed to us how important a symbol of hope for change the ordinations were to a great many people nationally and even internationally.

In the absence of an ELCA Lutheran bishop to sanction our ordinations, the three of us were blessed by an interfaith coalition of clergy and "extraordinarily" ordained by over forty ELCA clergy, which included the San Francisco Conference. After their blessing and the presentation of our stoles, we then moved from the altar to the center of the congregation to receive the people's blessing—those gathered in San Francisco, as well as those who stretched out their hands in blessing from communities across the country. A celestial choir, cloaked in light from the stained glass windows, sang from the loft. The pungent smell of incense lingered in the air over us. A liturgical dancer and a group of drummers rounded out this joyous celebration.

The high point of the service was the unexpected blessing—both terrifying and powerful—given to the three of us and to our preacher by the dancer. Carrying a wand of fire that he used to anoint us, the dancer cast its flame over each of our heads and before the mouth of our preacher, Carter Heyward. With that fiery blessing, the Holy Spirit was manifested in the eloquence of Carter's sermon. As priest and theologian at the Episcopal Divinity School in Cambridge, Massachusetts, Carter's own irregular ordination in 1974 had pioneered the way for ours in 1990. Years after our ordinations, we remember the fire of the Spirit, the witness of the Word, and the spiritual voltage of those blessings. They became the energy that powered us for the whole of our ministry.

Following our ordinations, the calling congregations of First United and St. Francis each received letters of commendation from Mayor Art Agnos and State Senator Milton Marks in recognition and support of their actions. Simultaneously, both congregations were brought up on charges of violating the constitution of the ELCA. Each had knowingly challenged ELCA policies by independently calling and ordaining the three of us: St. Francis by calling a committed lesbian couple and First United by calling a single gay man who steadfastly refused to promise lifelong celibacy. It would take another twenty-five years before marriage would become legal for lesbians and gay men throughout the United States.

Six months after our ordinations, the two congregations faced a "disciplinary hearing" by the ELCA, which was experienced as a trial by the accused. The case against the congregations was litigated by the ELCA's own prosecuting attorney. Thankfully, a civil attorney who was a member of St. Francis offered his legal services pro bono in defense of the two congregations. Neither congregation denied being in violation of the ELCA's constitution. They based their case on the necessity of being responsive to the time they were living in and the urgency of need surrounding them. In calling us, the congregations declared that full recognition of a population historically discriminated against within both church and society was not only right, but also long overdue.

The hearing was arbitrated by an ELCA disciplinary committee of eleven members. The ELCA had the right to pick two thirds of the committee from the national pool of names willing to serve on a disciplinary hearing panel. The congregations could select the remaining third. The disciplinary committee would function as both judge and jury. With the deck already seriously stacked against the congregations, Jeff, Phyllis, and I fully understood this public platform needed to count, regardless of the verdict. This was the first disciplinary hearing in the ELCA. It was open to the public, including journalists. In the next two decades, there would be four other disciplinary hearings on the same issue and eighteen more "extraordinary ordinations" in the ELCA of LGBT people. However, future prosecutions would target the "irregularly" ordained individuals rather than the congregations in support of them. Those hearings would be closed to both journalists and the public.

The three of us knew we would be called to testify for our congregations' defense. We each recognized that we carried the burden of giving voice to all those who were hostage to silent closets of fear and shame as well as those who had come out to their families and congregations only to be discounted or discarded. As I waited my turn to testify, I grew increasingly nervous thinking of this responsibility. Just before I took the stand, a woman slipped into my hand a small chip of what appeared to be concrete. She whispered, "I'd like to give you this. It's a piece of the Berlin Wall. I think that's what the three of you are about—knocking down walls." I held it as I gave my testimony. I was no longer afraid. I was inspired. As I heard my own voice, I knew it was a communal voice, uplifted by all those who were standing with us and represented by us.

At the hearing's conclusion, the two congregations were each given a sentence of suspension from the ELCA by a close vote of six to five. However, the verdict stated that after five years, the suspension would automatically convert to expulsion if the congregations remained in "noncompliance" with national church policy. By 1995, both congregations were indeed still noncompliant in retaining us and were subsequently expelled. The San Francisco Board of Supervisors responded by sending a letter of censure to the ELCA, in protest of the expulsion. Together, the two congregations had become the communal face of love in the city.

The following is a statement made after the trial by Mari Irvin, a congregational leader in our church community:

"I tell people, 'If you want to find an easy church to join, St. Francis Lutheran is not the one. However, if you want to be part of a family/community that shares something very powerful, then you are in the right place.' At St. Francis, I am fully accepted—*all* of me. As a member of this community I have become stronger and more affirmed in my experience of the love of God. I cannot express the collage of feelings I experienced on my first visit after having been away from the Christian Church nearly twenty years. God calls all of us to be servants who go out in good courage, not knowing where we will be going but trusting God's hand to guide us. As a congregation, St. Francis is also like that. We can't know the outcome of all that we are doing, but we are faithful, and we are not afraid. I am confident that in twenty-five years, people will look back and say that we were significant in changing attitudes in the wider Church. The Church operates on geological time. We must be both patient and persistent, like water on rock." [5]

Historically, fear of difference coupled with the prerogatives of privilege assumed by majority culture lay at the heart of refusing to see that full recognition of gay and lesbian people was a justice issue. Religious and social institutions had long normed homosexuality as a matter of aberrant and/or immoral behavior while at the same time paradoxically regarding homosexuality as a "sickness" that either needed to be "treated" or just couldn't be helped. As a result, gay and lesbian people became objects of condescending pity or targets for virulent hatred. By pathologizing gay and lesbian "patients" as mentally ill or having a developmental disorder, medical institutions could justify such treatments as chemical castration and electroshock aversion therapy. In this environment, attitudes toward LGBT people hardened into condemnation, rejection, criminalization, and prosecution, resulting in suicides and even murders.

Finally, in 1998, the American Psychiatric Association came out in opposition to any treatment based on assumptions of pathology or disorder, rejecting such treatments as both ineffective and dangerous. Despite this, as of 2018, conversion therapy remains legal in forty-one states. This "therapy" is intended to change the sexual orientation, gender identity, or gender expression of LGBT people.

According to a 2018 report out of the Williams Institute at UCLA School of Law, it is estimated that:

- 698,000 LGBT adults, ages eighteen to fifty-nine, in the US have received conversion therapy.
- 20,000 LGBT youth, ages thirteen to seventeen, will receive conversion therapy from a licensed health-care professional

before they reach the age of eighteen in the forty-one states that currently do not ban the practice.

- 57,000 youth, ages thirteen to seventeen, across all states will receive conversion therapy from religious or spiritual advisors before they reach the age of eighteen. [6]

Chillingly, the report goes on to say that laws banning conversion therapy do not apply to religious or spiritual advisors who engage in sexual orientation or gender identity change efforts within their pastoral capacity. Absent of legal accountability, religious institutions and their leaders carry a great deal of responsibility for the sufferings of LGBT people, while simultaneously having a unique opportunity to significantly ease those sufferings. As one gay man who had been in the military pointed out, "Only religious institutions claim power over us during our lives *and* into eternity. Even the military doesn't claim that much power. Why is it that power in the name of righteousness is so easily misused?"

Years after our divorce, I looked up my ex-husband when my advocacy work took me near his hometown for a speaking engagement. By then I had hopes that in the intervening years he had made peace with, and found happiness in, his gay identity as I had. Instead, he told me he had gone through Exodus, a self-avowed Christian "reparative therapy" program that professes to "cure" homosexuals. He acknowledged that he still had occasional "lapses" with men but dismissed them as insignificant because they were people he didn't know well or care about. When I asked, "Have you never allowed yourself to fall in love with any man you did care about?" he responded, "No, because it's easier to repent of lust than it is to repent of love." We parted, sadly aware we had taken very different paths with no bridge between them.

At St. Francis, one of our members spoke movingly of the trauma he experienced after "coming out" as gay to his parents in adolescence. Desperate to help their son and trusting the psychiatrist who recommended it, his parents institutionalized him, authorizing electroconvulsive shock treatment to help "reset" his heterosexuality. Remarkably, as an adult who later fully embraced his gay identity, this man was able to forgive his parents and resume a loving relationship with them despite the psychic and emotional scars this experience had left. He recounted that, as a widow in her old age, his mother had finally expressed her regret saying, "Son, I'm so sorry. We really did not understand what we were doing. In those days, everyone thought this was something that should be fixed. We were wrong. You're not a problem to be fixed. You're my son, and I love you. I'm just grateful that you are happy."

St. Francis and First United knew that shame could not be healed by the adoption of spirituality through the denial of sexuality. Shame can only be healed by respect coupled with love. When love holds all facets of personhood with unconditional regard, our humanity can be fully realized. When sexuality and soul, mind and body, spirit and intellect are celebrated as essential to our humanity, everyone has the potential to become whole. In knowingly calling a gay man who embraced his sexuality and an openly lesbian couple who celebrated theirs, the congregations had taken a public stance in opposition to their denomination's discriminatory policies and society's pejorative treatment of gay men and lesbians. For them it was an issue of justice-love. As a result of their actions, the congregations became public beacons of hope to countless souls still trapped in dark closets of fear and shame.

Through the years, what people have had difficulty understanding, or have not wanted to understand, is that homosexuality is not an issue of morality, nor is it a disorder, nor a lifestyle. It is fundamentally an issue of *identity* and *affinity* as fully as that of heterosexuality. What heterosexuality, homosexuality, and pansexuality all have in common is what everyone has in common: namely, that responsible expression of sexuality is fully realized within loving relationships of trust, respect, and mutuality. As LGBTQ young adults today succinctly put it, "However you identify, it's about hearts, not parts."

6

Hospitality in the Era of AIDS

St. Francis Lutheran Church was located in the heart of the city close to the Castro, a neighborhood that had become the epicenter of the AIDS virus. Our home was the parsonage provided by the congregation, but it was the community itself that became our home's foundation. The nearly century-old congregation had a well-earned reputation for reaching out to its neighbors and being involved in the challenges of city life. Built in 1905, and having survived the great earthquake of 1906, the congregation volunteered the church as an infirmary for six months for those injured in the quake and the fires that followed. This early beginning set a course for the congregation that continuously served the needs of the city as its neighborhood populations and their needs changed through the succeeding years.

At the time of our arrival in 1990, the highest percentage of people with HIV in the United States lived in the forty-nine square miles that was San Francisco. The city was reeling from the epidemic of HIV/AIDS before highly active antiretroviral therapy became available for treatment of the disease. Known for its progressive politics, its social tolerance, and its welcoming of diverse cultures, San Francisco had become an oasis of refuge to gay people who had been disenfranchised from home and family.

In fact, many of them were transplants from the more conservative Midwest. The opportunity to claim sexual freedom became a deadly conduit for the mysterious disease of HIV/AIDS.

As the crisis of AIDS continued to accelerate, many gay men were struggling with their own illness while in mourning for a partner who had already succumbed to his. It was a time when a diagnosis meant certain death within a matter of months to a couple of years. Strong young men rapidly became ghosts of their former selves. Many lost their entire support systems of friends and partners. Looking back, one gay man who suffered from survivor's guilt reflected sadly, "No one knew what was causing AIDS, and we were unprepared to handle sexuality responsibly. After spending years trying not to be gay, we were like kids in a candy store when we first experienced the freedom to live with abandon. I don't know how or why I lived as my friends died around me. I only know I stopped counting after fifty deaths."

Fear of transmission, combined with ignorance of the means of transmission, contributed to the scarcity of care for those who became ill. When it became thought of as an infectious "gay disease," fear and disgust attended it along with relief that it seemed to be confined to "that" population. But help came from an unlikely quarter. Lesbian women began to step up as caregivers to their gay brothers. This was a welcome surprise because in the earlier years of the epidemic, it was not unusual for many lesbian women and gay men to lead fairly separate lives from one another.

The saying "History is written by the victors" is no less true for religious history. Religious communities have historically tended to rely chiefly on male leaders and male imagery for Divine Presence. This has led to normalizing power as "higher and over" rather than valuing power as "within and together." Although both gay men and lesbian women shared the experience of oppression within the dominant culture, a god viewed as exclusively male still allowed gay men to identify with divine power but furthered the alienation and disempowerment of lesbian women. This was compounded by the limited roles for women's leadership in the Church and its institutions of learning. As a result, lesbians had little opportunity for spiritual fulfillment by affiliating with conventional religious communities.

As Phyllis and I began our work together in team ministry, we realized there was a naive expectation that adding us to the clergy team meant lesbians would naturally gravitate to becoming members of the parish. We had to help our congregation understand that expecting lesbians to embrace a liturgical tradition that strongly reflected the patriarchal side of its history was neither spiritually inviting nor hospitable. The congregation responded by wholeheartedly embarking on a journey of liturgical and theological self-awareness. They began to embrace the contributions of Jewish and Christian feminists within the worship experience. One of our clergy colleagues, Michael Hiller, used his poetic skills to artfully reframe the exclusive language and imagery in our prayers, creeds, and hymns until we had a modest library of inclusive liturgies we could draw upon for all our worship services. Lesbians, as well as heterosexual women, began to see their lives represented in the stories, symbols, music, and visual art reflected in our communal life and worship. They became valued as leaders as well as visible in service.

Guided in their vision by Senior Pastor James DeLange, the congregation clearly saw a parallel between their full inclusion of gay and lesbian people and the welcome Jesus freely extended to all who suffered on the margins of society. Indeed, the disease of AIDS and the fear it engendered had a parallel with the disease of leprosy in the time of Jesus. In reaching out to the gay community that was being so deeply affected by HIV/AIDS, the congregation understood that their work in the world was that of compassionate care together with persistent striving for justice. The stigma of AIDS on top of internalized homophobia from both church and society caused many people to be ashamed to live and afraid to die. For them, life was condemnation, staying or going. St. Francis was a needed refuge for healing the soul and integrating spirit with body. The people of St. Francis saw it as Jesus-work.

In 1993, the congregation sent a contingent of members to participate in the March on Washington for Lesbian, Gay, and Bi Equal Rights, and Liberation. Before the march, Phyllis and I decided to walk the Names Project Quilt memorializing the 129,491 people who had died of AIDS in the US from 1980–1993. [7] We thought of the many lives we had personally loved and lost in our first three years of living in San Francisco. Walking the quilt, we paused at a square in which people were writing new names. Phyllis bent down to add the names of those whom we had lost in our community. When she was done, we gazed out at this vast comforter of sorrow blanketing the Washington Mall. Through eyes blurred with tears, we watched the sky darken to a vivid violet. Standing under clouds swollen with raindrops, it felt like the heavens joined all of us in our mourning. As we took a path leading out of the quilt, we were caught up short by a square that had sewn into it these words: "There is a land of the living, and there is a land of the dead. The bridge is love, the ultimate meaning, the only survival." [8] That day, love and sorrow were inextricably entwined.

Back in San Francisco, we resumed our work. Along with the many tourists who came for sightseeing, there were other guests who arrived to grieve the imminent loss of their gay sons dying of AIDS in the city's hospitals. Our congregation was located within a block of a new residential hospice and the premier medical center for the treatment of people with AIDS. Recognizing the need for temporary housing for these grieving parents, the congregation made apartment units available in an adjacent building it owned. It then intentionally became the sort of spiritual community that enfolded its visitors in hospitality, offering emotional, spiritual, and practical support as needed. It also offered unequivocal love free from religious judgment. In short, it offered an experience of home amid spiritual community to parents who rarely dared hope for such loving care and understanding from their home communities.

Between the hospital, the hospice, and the congregation, Phyllis's spiritual care work both within and outside the church community kept her constantly busy at all hours. She and the San Francisco coroner were soon on a first name basis. He respectfully called her "The Angel of Death," so impressed was he by her sensitivity and skill at helping ease people's passage at time of transition and provide comfort to their surviving partners.

From parents we heard, "My home congregation doesn't even know why we're here. We couldn't tell them we have a gay son, let alone a son with AIDS. We never knew a church like this existed." One frail gay man who had been a visitor several times with his partner lingered after church to talk to us. He said, "I need a community in which to die, and my partner needs a community in which to grieve. We know churches that pity us because we are dying of AIDS but would not think to support us as a couple apart from AIDS. Yours is not like that. You honor our relationships in sickness and in health. You show us respect, not pity. We're glad to be here. We want to become members. After standing outside so long, we've finally come in. We're home."

Author's Note: As of 2018 in the US, there are 1.1 million people living with HIV. 692,790 people with AIDS have died since the beginning of the epidemic. There are approximately 38,500 new infections per year. [9]

Getting to Know Our Homeless Neighbors

In 1994, we moved into the old Mission-style parsonage that was attached to a childcare center the church had partnered with since its beginnings. The center served children who came from middle- and low-income households as well as children whose families had lost their homes or had family members who were incarcerated. In a block of yardless row houses, our building was unusual in that it had a small, untended, and overgrown front garden bordered by a low picket fence. We cleared out the trash and painted the fence, lacing it with vines of sunny nasturtiums. We then resurrected the garden, placed welcoming benches inside the unlocked fence, and let it be known around the neighborhood that our lemon tree was fair game for anyone to pick when the fruit was ripe.

Soon the childcare kids began pausing on their way into the center to enjoy the flowers or pick the fruit. Then they asked if they could plant their own little garden plot by the front entrance to the center. With additional help from parents and volunteers, the kids soon had their own plot by the front door, together with container gardens in the backyard playground.

Meanwhile, our front yard garden had become very popular with the public. Elders out walking paused to rest on the benches, as did homeless people who sometimes took short naps on them. Nervous neighbors worried that such hospitality would be a magnet to more homeless people and could cause trouble, and such fears were not unfounded. The homeless population, with their ubiquitous panhandling and numerous encampments, was a small town within the city, with approximately a thousand people encamped in Golden Gate Park alone.

The majority of the homeless population had lost their housing as the price of rent continued to rise and developers focused on new housing for upper-income residents. Other homeless people came from out of state, attracted to fair weather and generous public assistance, only to find they would more often than not be shut out of overcrowded shelters and rejected by overwhelmed treatment services. To help address the needs of homeless people, the congregation helped initiate an interfaith coalition of communities that offered hot meals, shelter, showers, clothing, food vouchers, and the availability of social workers and phones to assist in applying for jobs, training, and permanent housing.

Many homeless people did have problems with drugs and alcohol, and some began encamping at night in the generous walkway leading to a side entrance to the childcare center that was just below our flat. We got to know them first by their street names: Little Bear, Whiner, Jamaica, and the like. But when they were sober and had begun to trust us, they would share their real names and tell us their stories. Occasionally, we were able to reunite some of them with their families, but mostly, we just tried to *be* family to them as a spiritual community. Those who camped out in the walkway by the childcare center understood that they and their shopping carts filled with the necessities of street life survival needed to be gone before the childcare program opened in the morning. To safeguard the area, a volunteer from the congregation came every morning to sweep the walkway and check the garden area for refuse and dirty needles.

On warm nights, our regulars sometimes drank too much and talked too loud and too long before going to sleep. Late on one hot night, they woke our then five-year-old daughter, Noelle, whose bedroom window was open one floor above their encampment. Thoroughly annoyed, I leaned out the window, glared down at them, scolded them for waking her, and let them know that if they couldn't keep their noise down, I would call the police to move them out.

Shocked, my daughter exclaimed, "Mom! I only wanted you to ask them nicely if they could be quieter. Some of them are my friends!"

One such friend was a homeless man named Aaron who was a fixture outside our church. He regularly distributed a newsletter called *The Street Sheet* to passersby. This publication was written by homeless people to make sure the public saw them as having individual stories and identities. It kept visible those who had gotten work and were beginning to thrive and those who had died on the streets and deserved to be remembered in their passing. Sometimes it contained the raw poetry of the streets, giving the public a firsthand account of life under the freeway overpass or in tent encampments on the Civic Center Mall. Their newsletter was a way to say, "Look at me! I'm human. I have a story beyond what you see and what you think you know."

Living in such close proximity to the sometimes violent and often precarious life on the streets with its attending issues of addiction and mental illness, we felt we needed to safeguard our openhearted little girl as best we could. We set up "safe houses" for her in our neighborhood with merchants and residents. In the general population of the homeless street "regulars," we also trusted Aaron to look out for her, knowing his story from alcoholism to sobriety and having witnessed his own efforts to better his prospects. Their bond was undeniable. Whenever she spotted him, Noelle would run to him expecting a hug. He would scoop her up and twirl her around in a dancing embrace—his eyes alight and his toothless smile radiant with delight. To this day, she remembers him with affection.

Another homeless regular was a man who slept under the thickets of a wooded hillside behind the nursery school Noelle attended. The children saw him frequently when they were out using the playground equipment (under adult supervision) and accepted him as part of the landscape. He seldom spoke, and on the few occasions when he did, he was polite but quite disorganized in his thinking. Sometimes, after school hours, he would enter a small, unlocked kitchenette that had been added to the very old public facility leased to the school. The adults realized he was looking for coffee and began leaving out the leftover afternoon coffee for him to take back to his encampment.

We knew him as James. Seeing how thin he was, I let James know about our hot meals program at the church. He began showing up for meals. Then one Sunday, he attended service wearing a very tattered clergy chasuble draped over his street clothes. (A chasuble is an ornate outer vestment worn by the presiding clergyperson at the Eucharist on high holy days or festival Sundays.) When people were invited to come forward in small groups around the altar to receive Holy Communion, James came forward with great reverence and dignity. Kneeling at the altar rail, he extended his hand for the bread. Kneeling next to James, his hand outstretched as well, was Victor, a member of our parish who had both prestige and considerable wealth. Phyllis—also wearing a chasuble because she was the presider at this service—vividly remembers this study in contrasts:

"There they were together, each seeking the presence of Christ in their lives. Victor was used to rubbing shoulders with Washington lobbyists at various fundraisers. He even hand-delivered the St. Francis Cookbook to Hillary Clinton when she was first lady. But Victor's life changed after he knew he had AIDS and had only a limited time to live. Money and prestige no longer mattered to him. Giving became far more important. As I communed both James and Victor that day, I was struck by how we are all so much more connected to one another than we can ever know. Rich or poor, powerful or powerless, worn chasuble or pristine chasuble, we are all welcomed guests of God's hospitality."

Not long after, Phyllis sat at Victor's bedside holding his hand as he took his final breath. James continued to come to church wearing the chasuble, and no one batted an eye. Our parishioners understood that he was simply, in his own fashion, "dressed for church." They kept feeding him and merely smiled when he began signing our guest book as "the Pope."

Over time, it was clear, as it became increasingly dingy, that James was using the heavy chasuble as a coat for warmth at night as well. We made sure James had access to clean blankets and clothes as well as another congregation's lodging. But James preferred to live outdoors and continued to show up for Sunday service in his chasuble. In some religious circles this would have been considered an offense. But to us, it seemed fitting that a homeless man sheltering under the stars should derive comfort from a symbol of Christianity. We were certain that he was as deserving of it as any priest and that Jesus would have been the first to approve.

James continued to encamp near the school grounds. Late one night, a very distraught James dialed 911 to report that he had discovered some "dead babies" in the school's fireplace. He said he had tried to revive them but had not succeeded. When the police arrived they found James waiting for them in the main schoolroom. He had entered through a door the custodian had accidentally left unlocked. Inside they found three dolls that had been carefully laid on a baby blanket on the floor. Ringed around them were some orange pylons that were normally used to reserve parking for the teachers during school hours. James told the police that he had tried to shield the "babies" from harm and had done a blessing rite for them when he could not revive them.

The doll babies had indeed been sleeping in their toy cradles in a large fireplace niche that had been brightly painted over as a doll-sized room for them. But all James understood was that babies had died in that fireplace, and he had been unable to save them. The police did not arrest him, as the school had no interest in pressing trespassing charges. A short while later, James disappeared. We wondered if he had become so traumatized over the supposed deaths of those doll babies that he could no longer endure camping there. We never found out what happened to that troubled soul, nor did we learn much of his story while he was with us. But we were glad he was part of the community for a time, and we knew that, in God's eyes, he deeply mattered, and so he was one of us.

Family Ties Within Community

Living far away from our Midwest families of origin and busy in spiritual community, we turned our focus to many within our community and within our neighborhood who were also at a distance from family, through geography or rejection or bereavement or homelessness.

The congregation knew there was a sizable low-income senior population that lived around the church in the rent-controlled housing established years earlier. As the area grew more affluent, the congregation opened a senior center to offer support for elders they knew were struggling. Once a week, thirty to forty elders gathered for a hot meal followed by games, concerts, and urban field trips. There were conversations on the issues of the day coupled with meditations on spiritual practice. Resources were made available for medical care, housing, and grief support.

The childcare center children became regular visitors to the senior center so children and elders could enjoy each other's company through the shared pleasure of a hug, some story time, the gift of a crayon drawing, or a cookie for the road. Dances were also a big hit, especially the "seniors' prom," a noontime affair that included a festive luncheon followed by a dance with live music. Since many of our elders were widowed women, the gay men in the congregation and in the neighborhood took long lunch hours to attend the prom. They arrived dressed to the nines, bearing flowers for their senior dance partners. Unanticipated family relationships began to form between young and old, gay and straight, and members and visitors to the congregation. Caregiving groups began coalescing around shared meals and friendship.

Once a month, Wednesday evenings at the church were dedicated to Community Night, a program for low-income children and their parents or guardians who had few ties to supportive communities. Before supper, members of the congregation volunteered to help cook or assist children with their homework. The meal was served at candlelit tables with fresh flowers. Parents were invited to bring their little ones in pajamas so that sleepyheads could doze and be more easily carried home to bed. There was always a child-centered activity after supper, followed by a child-friendly, optional Eucharist in the sanctuary.

The children called the downstairs meal in the parish hall the "meal for our stomachs" and the upstairs meal in the sanctuary the "meal for our hearts." Since most of the families in this program were not affiliated with religious communities, it surprised us that they participated in the upstairs meal almost as much as the downstairs meal. One evening, a mother told me apologetically that she and her child would be leaving after supper. As I was assuring her that was fine, her child piped up, "*Mom*, we can't skip the meal for the heart—that's the *important* one!" The mother looked at me, smiled, and said, "I guess we're staying."

When we shared the upstairs meal, we all sat on the rug in the chancel, gathered in a circle around the child-sized altar placed below the high altar. Standing above us in a niche in the wall was a statue of Jesus, his arms extended over us in blessing. After sharing the bread and grape juice symbolizing the promise of his abiding love, we walked to the back of the church where the life-sized angel holding a baptismal shell knelt. Close to the angel was a prayer screen with votive candles. Gathered around at eye level with the kneeling angel, the children were invited to share any concerns they had or light a candle for anyone they were thinking about before we concluded our evening with prayer. It was deeply moving and often troubling to hear their adult-sized concerns: bullying in school, gangs after school, a parent dying of cancer, or loneliness for an incarcerated family member. Sometimes we were able to accomplish effective interventions, but more often we could only offer prayerful hearts and a safe, loving place in this moment of their lives.

One mom who attended Community Night with her two daughters was an administrative assistant at the childcare center the congregation helped to support. Jade gave this account of how she and her two daughters became participants in Community Night: "One day after I had picked up Chloe from school and we were walking home, we came to a storefront that had a poster in the window alerting the public to a missing child. We stopped to study her photo and read the description. It gave me chills to realize that child was the same age as mine. The poster called on volunteers to join the hunt for her. Chloe studied it silently and then asked me a question I didn't know how to answer: 'Who would look for me if I were missing, Mom?' That's when I decided we needed to come to Community Night. I figured if this church was a safe place for gay men with AIDS, it was the right place for us too." As we listened, we were honored that this mother looked to us for reassurance of loving community. That evening, we knew we had been given two children to hold as a sacred trust.

A few years later, the congregation supported Chloe in a study abroad program, nurturing her into young womanhood and being extended family to her and her sister when her mother was terminally ill with cancer. As Phyllis and I visited with Jade at her bedside not long before she died, Jade paused in our conversation to ask if we could see the "other people" in the room with her or if they were just for her to see. We indicated they were for her eyes to see, and she replied calmly, "Oh, that's okay then. They sometimes come and go, like they're checking on me."

At the close of our visit, we asked if we could give her a blessing, together with her daughters. Jade agreed, saying, "I cherish your blessing and the gift of your love. When I came to St. Francis, it was to give my daughters a community that would find them if they were ever lost. But in providing for them, *I* got a community that gave me a safe place to wrestle with God. And now I am receiving the blessing of care at the end of my life. I could go to sleep tonight and not wake up, and it would be all right."

After we blessed her, she proceeded to bless all of us gathered at her bedside as well. Lingering over her two daughters, Jade traced her fingers over their brows, marking them with love to carry on without her. As I think about this experience today, I am reminded of a line from the poet Elizabeth Barrett Browning: "When light is gone, love remains for shining." [10]

Increasingly, the church was becoming that place of gathering where people both look out for one another and celebrate each other. If someone had a baby, the Lydia circle, a group of gay men in drag, hosted the shower and added their festive touch and outrageous humor to the occasion. If one in our midst succumbed to AIDS, the community gathered first to care for him and after death to bury his ashes beneath a stone engraved with his name in the Garden Memorial Terrace alongside the church. Each year their names would be read aloud on the festival of All Saints.

What became evident to us the longer we stayed in ministry in San Francisco was that the depth of sorrow our congregation sustained was equaled by its capacity for joy. In those circumstances, all of life is lived closer to the bone and closer to the heart. When we grieve deeply, we need the company of those who have lived through those depths and know the way forward, because the way back is gone. They are the ones who will sit in the dark with a fellow sufferer and then gently crack the blinds so tear-filled eyes can slowly become accustomed to the light, one sliver at a time.

At St. Francis Lutheran Church, this traveling blessing is offered at the close of the Eucharist: "Live in forgiveness, claim your wholeness, and go in peace." Love invites us to live wholly so that we may die whole. It was in those sorrow-filled, joyful, and challenging years serving this small community with a big heart that our concept of hospitality and home came together. It was formed in the crucible of AIDS, the crisis of urban homelessness, and the unjust plight of LGBT people in church and society. The miracle of life was not lost on our congregation. It did not grow numb with despair. The spirit of our congregation was as hopeful as its love was deep, a miracle only time and faith in Holy Presence can grow.

Two Moms, Two Dads, and One Baby

A year into ministry, we realized we had become so immersed in community that we had neglected to take time to establish friendships in San Francisco. We had also neglected to check in with each other regarding a conversation begun before our move about starting a family of our own.

In Minneapolis, we had taken a "Maybe Baby" class for lesbians who were considering parenting. It was now time to resume the conversation. A couple of relationship breakups within our circle of friends in Minneapolis had encouraged us to invest more deliberately in our San Francisco friendships. After one such breakup following a visit from a Minneapolis couple particularly dear to us, we despondently cast about for people who might become friendship possibilities in San Francisco.

A gay male couple we had recently met came to mind. We had both noted their relaxed way with one another and their easy banter. Impulsively, we called them up, explained our sudden need for the diversion of low spirits, and invited them over for coffee just to talk to us about the reasons they liked being together. Surprised by the request but cheerfully agreeing, they arrived at our door a half hour later, dressed in matching zippered jackets—mischievous smiles playing across their faces. At the door, Jay asked, "This visit is for healing, right?" I nodded an affirmative. "Well, Ched, I think we wore the right thing." With that, they both unzipped their jackets to reveal crystals hanging by ribbons around their necks, plucked from their dining room chandelier. "Because we heard lesbians are into crystals for healing," Jay explained. Who could resist such silliness? We were instantly bonded in friendship. Little did we guess that we had just met the fathers of our future child.

In the months ahead, they continued to win our hearts with their good humor and satisfy our stomachs with delicious meals. Their home became our oasis of respite from the endless demands of intense but meaningful ministry. Yet it wasn't until the four of us began camping together that conversations became wide-ranging and more serious. Weathering rain-soaked tents and snow in the Sierra Mountains tested our camping chops and everyone's good humor but did not dim our enthusiasm for adventuring together. It was over a campfire by the Russian River north of San Francisco that we first cautiously broached the subject of "what if" we became parents together. At that time we knew such an unorthodox arrangement could not be founded upon any legally binding ties for the four of us. It required quite a leap of faith to count on a lifetime of family connection to one another and many more discussions over the next two years to reach a definitive decision. But by December of 1992, we had all committed to "the mission," as Jay mischievously named it, dubbing the two of them as "the support staff" to the mission. By January of 1993, the mission was accomplished! Phyllis was pregnant with our daughter.

Taking advantage of some time off before the birth, Phyllis and I returned to Minnesota for a much-needed vacation to see our families and friends. By this time, Phyllis was visibly pregnant. To enjoy a slower pace, we decided we would spend the greater part of our time at our family lake cabin where Phyllis could get some rest in the secluded and peaceful Minnesota Northwoods. A section of the lake that had several properties owned by Lutheran pastors had become known as "Preachers' Point." Because of the publicity surrounding our ordinations and the subsequent trial, we had become well-known in the ELCA nationally. We used to joke that we were having our "fifteen minutes of infamy" which meant we never quite knew what kind of reception we might receive in Lutheran circles at any given time. For most of our week, we managed to avoid Preachers' Point.

Toward the end of our Northwoods stay, we took the canoe out once more, savoring the last evening of our vacation. As we approached Preachers' Point on the way back to our cabin, the sun was setting, turning the placid lake molten gold. From a distance, we noticed a man standing at the end of his long dock who appeared to be staring at us for several minutes. Suddenly, he began waving his hat and called out, "Come here." Reluctantly, we turned the canoe toward his dock. He kept urging us to "come closer, come closer." As we drew closer, I recognized him as the patriarch of one of our prominent Lutheran families, several of whose members were well-known pastors like him.

We finally hovered in the water just a few feet from him, wondering what was about to transpire. He said, "You're Phyllis Zillhart and Ruth Frost, aren't you?" When we said we were, he then spoke of the importance of our work and how needed it was in the Church. He acknowledged the trial and said, "What you do, you do for my granddaughter. She's lesbian too. Even if you never see the results of your work, *she* will. I want to bless you and your ministry." Then, noticing that Phyllis was pregnant, he added, "And your child too." He stretched his arms out wide over the water and gave us a beautiful blessing. We no longer remember the exact words. What we remember is his face shining gold like the water, his white hair waving gently in the light breeze, his voice strong and bold. In that moment, I recalled my father's blessing, given to us when he was dying and we thought our dreams of ministry were over. Here it was again, his vision embodied, a ringing reminder of grace and the power of resurrection. And the child was on her way.

Back in San Francisco, the time had come to meet our daughter. I rushed Phyllis to the hospital birthing center following a late-day work meeting we had both attended. We arrived at the hospital just as her amniotic fluid broke. The next day, Noelle was born with all four of us on hand to greet her. Later that day, I ran home to get some things we needed for discharge the following day.

At home, I was rummaging around in our office space and noticed a slip of paper drift slowly down to the floor in front of me. Picking up the scrap, I saw my father's elegant handwriting with these words on it: "Ruth Mary, you've given us a hummer today." Stunned, I immediately recalled our last conversation when I told him about our intention to have a child. I have no idea how that message came to me. I know the phrase stems from my childhood habit of humming at the table whenever my mother cooked something I loved. I know, too, that my father, hearing me, would sometimes look at my mother and smile and say, "Dear, I think you've cooked a hummer today." So the message had to have been a reference to a much earlier time in my life. But the fact that the message addresses *me*, together with the timing of its delivery, remains a mystery to this day. I have no recollection of having received or seen it earlier, nor what I may have given my parents to elicit this message. But somehow, it was "redelivered" to me at our child's birth. The lesson I take from it is this: Love has traveling power. Its messages are not bound by space or time if we have eyes to see and ears to hear.

When I returned to work several days later, I was told that someone from the religious right had called the church office three times to inquire if it was true that we were parents and that we had artificially inseminated with a gay male couple. When asked the motivation for this inquiry by our protective office manager, the caller said he "just wanted to check the facts to make sure this wasn't a grand hoax being perpetrated by the gay community." She responded that it was neither a hoax nor was it being perpetrated by anybody but was, in fact, a gift being celebrated within our congregation and the gay community associated with it. A few weeks later, the community gathered to celebrate Noelle's baptism. They immediately recognized the importance of their role to the little one who would spend her childhood in their nurturing embrace.

As we continued to grow our family-of-the-heart bond with Jay and Ched, we drew upon safe havens for lesbian and gay people, first through our loving congregation and then through support groups for lesbian and gay people and their children. But even in San Francisco, notable for its tolerance of diversity, we couldn't protect our child from being bullied at school. Because she shielded us from knowing how bad it was, we were pretty clueless for far too long. The school Noelle attended was known for its academic excellence. However, the students were principally Chinese and Russian immigrants whose families had recently come from countries that either denied the existence of gay people in their society or criminalized them. Noelle's good education came at a cost. "I stood up for you every day in school," our daughter later reported to us of her elementary school days.

I usually drove Noelle to school in the mornings, and after dropping her off, I would sometimes treat myself to coffee at a local coffee shop near her school. I noticed that among the "regulars" was a lone elderly Chinese man who used the house newspaper to try to improve his English. This meant he would frequently ask other customers for help when he encountered something he couldn't understand. Some were good about it. Others just tried to look busy, which was harder to do before the era of portable electronic devices. One day after watching him approach several people who didn't want to be bothered, he looked my way, and I knew it was my turn to help. He sat down with me and I explained the political editorial he was trying to read, going over many of the words with him. When we were done he thanked me and rose, turned to the other customers, and announced happily, "She so smart!" I was on his radar from then on.

Not long after this, Phyllis had a rare free morning and wanted to come along with us, suggesting we all treat ourselves to a muffin at the coffee shop before school. As we sat in the crowded coffee shop, Phyllis noticed three police officers standing on the fringe of the seating area, coffee cups in hand, waiting for a table to open up. Phyllis went around to three tables that had a free chair and gathered them up for the officers so they could sit while they waited.

Out of the corner of my eye, I saw the Chinese man whom I had befriended get up from his table and head our way. He stopped at our table and, pointing at each of us in turn, exclaimed first to Phyllis, "You so nice," then to me, "You so smart," and finally to Noelle, "You so pretty." We thanked him and then he asked Phyllis, "She your daughter?"

Phyllis replied, "Yes, she is." Motioning to include me, Phyllis added, "We are both her moms. She has two mothers." He furrowed his brow, confused (while I sat there thinking, *Really, Phyllis? You're going to get into this here?*). Touching my shoulder, Phyllis continued, "We live together. We are partners."

He replied, "What that?" My stomach tightened as the room went completely silent. I could see newspapers being slowly lowered as people waited to hear what Phyllis would say next.

"It's like we're married."

"I not understand," he said, looking at the three of us. As Phyllis was about to reply, he raised his hand as though to stop her and said brightly, "It not matter. You *family!*" And then he withdrew.

You could feel the collective exhale in the room as everyone relaxed, some smiling and nodding at us as they returned to reading their papers. This experience showed me that sometimes kindness has the power to overcome complex social concepts and even cultural bias. In essence, our Chinese friend was saying he didn't need or want to know more. He already knew enough. He recognized what was important. We were family to one another.

Each year Noelle accompanied us in the Freedom Day Parade, proud that her mothers had once been selected to be grand marshals of the parade and had even gotten to ride in a red Cadillac convertible. She loved riding on floats and always happily waved at everyone lining the sidewalks along Market Street to cheer on thousands of gay folks and our allies. As for me, I could never have dreamed six years earlier that I would go from watching a Gay Pride parade from the shadows of my closet to leading the largest Pride parade in the world as one of its grand marshals. Neither the miracle nor its irony was lost on me.

One year, Noelle learned about a very small gathering (about two hundred people at best) that would be walking somberly down Market Street in remembrance and protest of the abuse and violent deaths committed against transgender people. When I told her why the walk was taking place and how greatly misunderstood and persecuted they were, Noelle said, "Why don't we march with them?" I agreed we should, and the two of us joined a small gathering of transgender people and a handful of their allies.

Noelle was conspicuous for being the only child walking in the gathering and so was greeted warmly by the trans population. Sensing the serious mood of the walkers, she immediately asked if she could join those in the lead so she could help them carry their large banner. I nervously agreed, worried by what I knew could be the turnout of some hostile bystanders. But with the help of a police escort, the walk took place without incident. When we said goodbye at the end of the walk, she received grateful hugs from her new trans friends. And I received their thanks for bringing my child along, though it was really *she* who had brought *me*. That night, I watched the news coverage of the walk. There was our eight-year-old girl, standing in the center of the first row of people, her arms proudly linked with those carrying the banner.

Embracing Transitions Together

One day a young man stopped by the church and asked to see one of the pastors. He had a story to tell and a request to make. This account is based on his story as he told it to me and as we went on to live another chapter of it in our church community. It is the story of a child and her family.

From a very young age, Anne Marie knew she was different. As she grew, she found herself at odds with her life as it was defined for her by the Roman Catholic Church and by society. In mid-adolescence, knowing she was attracted to girls, not boys, Anne Marie "came out" as lesbian. Her courage to declare herself inspired her older brother to come out as gay and claim his identity openly as well. The two became supports for one another.

Anne Marie's family gradually adjusted to this new understanding of two of their family members. As time passed, Anne Marie enjoyed being able to date and have girlfriends. However, she began to have a growing awareness that adopting lesbian identity still did not fully match her own sense of self. Now a young adult, Anne Marie persisted in self-formation, realizing that "she" was not lesbian but that *he* was transgender. For a second time, Anne Marie came out to the family.

This became a catalyst for another member of the family. Witnessing his child's emergent self-identity and the determination and courage it took to claim it, Anne Marie's father realized he could no longer keep holding his own secret. He proceeded to come out as gay to his wife and children. Once again, the family had to reconfigure and redefine their family bond accordingly.

Anne Marie began hormone treatment for transitioning to living life as a trans man. Recognizing the importance of a name change for her "new" brother, Anne Marie's sister suggested the name "Joshua" of Hebrew Scripture. That Joshua was famous for having captured the ancient city of Jericho by circling the city and knocking down its walls with the clarion call of trumpets. She pointed out that Anne Marie had also knocked down walls within their family in order to claim a new self-understanding among them. And so Anne Marie became Joshua to his family and friends. When he and I met, Joshua had made the decision to have gender reassignment surgery (now more appropriately called gender affirmation surgery). By that time Joshua had left the Catholic Church behind along with his old gender identity. But he had not left behind his faith.

While Joshua was grateful for his family's willingness to take this journey with him, he realized he needed something else in preparation for the surgery that would reintegrate him with his emergent identity. He needed to know if his baptism still held and he needed to be sure that God knew him and blessed him. "Do I need to be rebaptized in order to be renamed?" he asked. I assured him he did not. But I suggested that we have a "ritual of thanksgiving for new beginnings," together with an affirmation of baptism under his new name. And so our preparations began. In a conversation with Joshua's mother, she sighed and said, "Pastor Ruth, all I wanted was an ordinary family."

I replied, "Yes, that would certainly have been easier. But you don't get *ordinary*. You get *extraordinary*." And they were, because through all their family reconfigurations, the one certainty this family maintained was their love for one another. Their love held fast as walls tumbled down around them and between them and within them. They were all reconfiguring their family bond around authenticity as well as love. They dared to believe that if they allowed love to lead, understanding would follow.

Joshua came from a very musical family who had sung together under the direction of their father, a choir director. The family decided to sing Joshua into a new song to celebrate his reunion with himself and with them as a trans man. They chose a call and response song whose theme was God calling Joshua out of the wilderness and leading him into a new land as one who was tearing down walls with the power of his song. Joshua worried that his voice would crack because of his hormone treatments and that he might slide between his old soprano voice and his new tenor voice. His family assured him his voice would still carry.

Joshua's sister made the altar cloth for the ritual. She had sewn seven trumpets into it, representing each member of their family and the Biblical Joshua. Joshua's mother had kept the original baptismal candle presented to Anne Marie and said she would bring it so we could relight it in celebration of his new identity.

On the day of the ritual, friends, family, coworkers, and congregants packed the church. Just before the service started, Joshua's mother ran up to me, excitedly waving a box that contained the candle presented in baptism years earlier to Ann Marie. Pulling it out of the box, she exclaimed, "Look, it was never lit! Today we will light it for the first time for Joshua! God has always known this day would come!"

And light it we did. Trumpets sounded, and Joshua's family choir called him home to himself and to them. He responded with a voice that carried clearly over the others. God called a son out of the wilderness, and the community and his family rejoiced to receive him. After the service, his father remarked, "There are some who would say that what we did here today was sacrilegious. But I believe that what we experienced together was truly sacred."

"Yes," I replied, "today, Joshua sang the song in his heart that is making him whole."

As everyone celebrated with Joshua and his family in the parish hall over cake and coffee, I discovered I was sitting next to Joshua's boss. He remarked, "You know, I never really understood any of this when Josh came out at work as transgender. When Josh invited me and his coworkers to this celebration, I really didn't want to come. But I also didn't want him to have a hard time at the office, so I thought I should set a good example. But now I get it! I will never forget this service. I am going back to the office and mandating that we all get ourselves educated about how to have a work culture where transgender people can feel welcome and safe." As I affirmed his intentions, I thought to myself, *It isn't just Joshua who has transformed.*

Wedding Bells and Other Miracles

With society forbidding same-gender couples to marry and have legal standing in the courts, it was easy for the Evangelical Lutheran Church in America—and most other mainstream church bodies—to follow suit in withholding unions in their sanctuaries. In this respect, many otherwise social-justice-minded religious organizations failed to lead society but rather followed it, sometimes at quite a distance. By withholding the same blessing of relationships accorded to heterosexual couples, mainstream churches didn't have to acknowledge or respect gay couples. But not to be acknowledged and respected is to be rendered first invisible and then expendable within majority culture. It was for good reason that "Silence = Death" became the rallying cry of AIDS activists and others working for LGBT rights.

To everyone's astonishment, on February 13, 2004 (Valentine's Day weekend), a miracle occurred in San Francisco. The city, long a sanctuary for many disenfranchised populations, threw open the doors to City Hall and began issuing marriage licenses to same-sex couples at the order of then Mayor Gavin Newsom. Newsom believed the California Constitution's equal protection clause authorized him to grant same-sex marriage licenses. He cited the catalyst for his decision as having heard then President George Bush, in his 2004 State of the Union Address, express support for a federal constitutional amendment to prevent same-sex marriage. [11]

Within hours of Newsom's action, hundreds of gay couples had dropped everything and sprinted to City Hall, hoping to be among the five hundred people the system could process daily. (The system consisted of six slow computers set up to issue amended gender-neutral licenses.) Like many couples with children, we quickly pulled our daughter, Noelle, out of her fourth-grade class so she could be present at our wedding. At City Hall, it was as though a fire alarm had sounded in reverse. Couples were running *into* the building as fast as they could. As the line of eager couples formed and began snaking around the rotunda and out the door, it continued for blocks. Couples came in their street clothes, hauling along strollers and babies. The air was electric with anticipation and excitement. There were many lusty rounds of "Goin' to the Chapel and We're Gonna Get Ma-a-a-rried" sung to the reporters covering the event. Among us were a handful of bemused straight couples who found themselves in a sea of friendly LGBT couples.

As it became clear that the wait for most of us would be several hours standing in line, people began freely chatting with those in front and behind them. Children began linking up and playing together in the halls and then returning to their parents in line, complaining of hunger. People began spontaneously sharing whatever food they had up and down the line—mostly PowerBars, water bottles, peanuts, and champagne. As time passed and the news got out, many citizens signaled their support by spontaneously bringing both heartier food and flowers for those waiting in line. Somehow, it was all enough. People saved spaces for anyone who had to join other lines leading to the restrooms. After four hours of waiting, a sympathetic adult remarked to Noelle, "You're very patient. You must be getting a little annoyed with the wait." Noelle replied, "All I am is excited for my moms."

Phyllis was there in clergy collar to hold up the professional side of our lives, and I was without collar to hold up the personal side, having made her promise to marry me first before she officiated at any weddings. Phyllis had no choice but to break that promise as people saw her collar and begged her to marry them while standing in line. There were actually three lines: one for licensing, one for ceremonies, and a third for recording them in the registrar's office. Given the shortage of clergy for such a crowd, I happily released her from her promise.

Most of the marriages were taking place at three stations in the gallery of the hall's rotunda at the top of the grand central staircase. Gradually, word got out that more clergy and more members of the board of supervisors were needed to keep pace with the crowd of waiting couples. One member of the board ran in, took one look at the crowd, and exclaimed, "This is marriage triage! Scrub me up, give me a gown, and I'm good for the day!"

When we finally reached the head of the ceremonies line, Supervisor Bevan Dufty—recognizing us from our public advocacy work—threw his arms around us and whispered, "Would you like to be married in the Board of Supervisors' Chambers? It's a beautiful space." We readily agreed, knowing that the room was associated with the history of the earliest "out" gay political pioneer, Supervisor Harvey Milk. A gay male couple whom Phyllis had already married while they were in line accompanied us as our witnesses, together with a lesbian couple who had been their witnesses but had not yet said their vows. Having salvaged a discarded floral bouquet that was still in good shape, Noelle offered to be their flower girl as well as ours. While Phyllis and I said our vows, Noelle stood between us, our arms around her as we clasped hands with each other. It was a very sweet moment for the three of us. After the lesbian couple had said their vows, Noelle pelted all of us with flower petals as we shared hugs. We laughed thinking about what oddly wonderful wedding albums we would have.

We left the same way every couple did after taking their vows, descending the two-story, forty-five-step grand central staircase of the rotunda. This beautiful marble staircase, covered in red carpet in celebration of love for Valentine's Day, led down to the main floor entryway with its magnificent wrought iron doors adorned in gold leaf. This gave each couple time to savor their slow descent on the elegant runway, accompanied by the welcoming applause of all those waiting their turn below. Anticipation among strangers had turned into celebration among friends. By the end of that day, Mayor Gavin Newsom had lost his voice and simply had to listen to the crowd chanting, "Thank you, thank you, thank you!" at him.

Once outside City Hall, we stopped for a moment to gaze at a statue of Lincoln on a pedestal near the entrance. Lincoln was depicted as seated in serious contemplation. Noelle stepped up and gently placed the last rose from our wedding bouquet in his partially open hand. Somehow, that simple gesture seemed to lighten his demeanor. Couples passing by smilingly nodded their approval. It had certainly felt like one more step toward freedom for all. The great wound left twenty-six years earlier by the assassinations of Supervisor Harvey Milk and Mayor George Moscone had finally been healed. There hadn't been so many queer people in City Hall since that sad event. It was a blessing to gather in hope and joy instead of sorrow and rage.

That night we arrived home tired but still riding the wave of marital bliss. We called Noelle's dads, hoping they could join us in a celebratory drink, but could not reach them. Casting about for others to call, we thought of our neighbors Jim and Jennifer, a couple who lived across the street. We called only to find that Jim had already gone to bed. We told Jennifer not to wake him and that we would talk to them the next day.

Calming down a bit, we decided we would simply celebrate together and make the rest of our calls to friends and family the following day. Twenty minutes later the bell rang, and there were Jim and Jennifer holding a bouquet of flowers, a box of chocolates, and a bottle of sparkling apple cider. Jim's hair was still tousled from sleep, but both were smiling. Needless to say, the friendship we had been cultivating together was cemented that evening.

When Noelle returned to school the following Monday, she excitedly announced our marriage, thinking that surely her class would then understand that we were "normal" people. Sadly, even her best friend, a tender-hearted Chinese American child, gasped, "Didn't you try to *stop* them?" In fact, one month later, the Supreme Court of California did stop them. The court ordered the county of San Francisco to enforce the existing marriage statutes and to refrain from issuing marriage licenses. On August 12, 2004, the California Supreme Court voided all the marriages. [12] However, the joy of that day remains indelible in memory. It would be another decade before same-gender-parented families would begin regularly receiving support coupled with legal protections. But that day, the dam of justice was breached, and the trickle of water that escaped turned into a mighty river no dam could ultimately contain. Following the flood of City Hall marriages, St. Francis hosted a service of blessing and a celebratory wedding reception for newly married couples and their families.

As time passed, St. Francis realized they had become an anticipatory community: one unafraid to live into a more just future simply by living it in the present. In essence, the congregation modeled what they prayed the ELCA would become. In the meantime, they would stand in as witnesses of hope for LGBT populations and all who were living on the margins of church and society. They did not do this alone. There were a handful of courageous, forward-looking congregations living the future in the present, but it took time for momentum and courage to gather and multiply.

In 2009, another miracle occurred: the present caught up with the future. Nineteen "patient and persistent" years after the disciplinary hearing in 1990, the Evangelical Lutheran Church in America repealed its discriminatory policy requiring gay people to pledge lifelong celibacy if they wished to serve in ministry. With this decision, the ELCA became the largest denomination in the US to welcome gay people into ordained ministry under the same terms as straight people. In 2011, the ELCA invited both St. Francis Lutheran Church and First United Lutheran Church back into the ELCA. The congregations graciously accepted the invitation. Remarkably, these milestones occurred prior to the 2015 ruling of the Supreme Court legalizing same-gender marriage.

The ELCA had at last demonstrated its ability to be responsive to the social evolution of LGBT rights. In so doing, it advanced the cause of justice-love taken up nineteen years earlier by two small congregations and their allies who had given that cause voice and vision. Ironically, the prosecuting attorney for the ELCA in the 1990 trial became a supportive member of a second congregation that voted in 1999 to call Jeff Johnson as their pastor. These welcome developments are testimony to the fact that, with time and willingness, anyone can change, and deep wounds can begin to heal.

The day of our City Hall marriage ranks among the purest experiences of unadulterated joy we have ever had, together with our "extraordinary" ordinations, the birth of our daughter, Noelle, and most recently, our grandson, Ciel. The adage "It takes a village to raise a child" was quite literally true for our daughter who, a mother herself now, looks back in gratitude for the presence of loving community in her life. For her parents, the experience of raising our child within its embrace has underscored the belief that wherever we live, "home" finds its anchor within loving communities and the families of choice and nurture we create in each locale. The day of our marriage, the entire city of San Francisco became the village. But we left our hearts in one small congregation within it that offered us home.

In keeping with its first century of service to the city of San Francisco, St. Francis Lutheran Church modeled hospitality and refuge, key characteristics that make a house a home, especially if it understands itself as a house of God. Simply put, wherever we are and however far we have traveled, *love is the way home.*

Making Living Spaces Loving Places

How does a house become your home? For us, it began with stories and trees. The woodwork in our 1925 home is made from oak. Its distinctive grain suggests wood that was cut from older growth forests. Alfred and Eleanor, the previous homeowners, lived here with their six children for fifty-five years. Their house was well used and lovingly cared for. Alfred particularly looked after the wood, polishing it to a burnished glow. We obtained a photo of Alfred and Eleanor from their son to honor their care of the home that had become ours after their deaths.

When we bought the property, there was only one tree on it. Their son tells of the day his father came home and proudly showed his family their reward for opening an account with the local bank: a tiny oak sapling. Together, the family ceremoniously planted the little tree in the middle of their large backyard. Now a towering tree with a forty-five-inch girth, its generous canopy provides shelter to our patio and home to many birds and squirrels that like to scold our dog from a safe distance.

Oak floors under our feet support us in our comings and goings and reflect both beauty and resilience. In this home, we live within the past life of trees. While the hearth is the heart of our home, we are forever connected to the hardwood forests of Northern Minnesota. Today, six new trees grace our property, keeping company with their elder. Residing in the same block as ours, Alfred's son keeps the stories of our home's past alive for us. While we are making new stories, we preserve the old and give thanks for the continuity of love.

We live in this house, acknowledging the past while abiding in the present, mindful that we are custodians of its future. Through the passage of time, it has become home to four families. This house holds their stories as it embraces our story. Daily, we live under its sheltering hospitality. And sometimes, as we listen to the wind blow through the big oak, we hear the house breathe.

~ Ruth Frost, *Journal Memories*

12

Homing with Children

If the greatness of a society can be measured by how it treats its most vulnerable populations, then the same applies to families. The measure of a family can be taken by how well adults treat their children. Little ones also observe and overhear how adults treat one another. While physical violence is clearly destructive, yelling and name-calling between adults undermines children's safety too. When adults disregard and mistreat their partners, children instinctively know they are next in line for similar treatment.

If we must be the change we wish for the world, so too must we be the kind of adults we wish for our children. If we are counting on our children to "do as we say, not as we do," then every rule we give them and every lesson we teach will be pointless. Children rarely do as we say if we are not modeling the behaviors we want to teach. As they grow up, chances are they will recycle our mistakes if we give them little else to emulate.

The awareness of children starts with our babies before they even have language. They learn whether it's safe to be held, whether someone will comfort them when they cry, whether basic needs will be met, whether their feelings are respected, whether their bodies are properly tended. They learn who they are and the depth of their value by how they are treated. They learn all this before they can put anything into words.

Because babies and young children are completely dependent on their caregivers, they deserve respect for their feelings as well as their bodies from the adults who tend them. This means adults must practice thoughtful observation and careful listening in order to understand their babies' physical and emotional cues. Is playtime that begins as peekaboo moving from a natural startled reaction to an escalating fear response? Whose benefit is being served when an adult continues to toss a young one about after their initial delight turns to tears? Has a tickle that elicits some harmless giggles morphed into sustained hysterical laughter because the child simply cannot control what is happening to them? These examples illustrate how easily we can overlook our young ones' cues. While they may seem minor, they are relevant in that they underscore how dependent our little ones are on our ability to read them and make adjustments in our behavior accordingly. The power lies entirely with us.

In our family, autonomy, creativity, and safety were important issues in parenting. We tried to practice love and boundaries, coupled with the acknowledgment that parents make mistakes just as their children do. Exploring her own autonomy came naturally to our daughter. As a young child, the words that would best describe Noelle are creative, spirited, and impulsive. She was physically agile and confident, and she enjoyed testing her abilities to their limits.

When Noelle was a toddler walking the busy streets of San Francisco, she developed the disconcerting habit of yanking her hand out of mine and dashing into any street that had something on the other side that she felt beckoned to her. Admonishments simply rolled off her. After the third dangerous incident, in desperation I decided to spank her. I stepped into a private parking lot and gave her three good swats. A steely look of resolve came over her face and I could clearly tell she was willing herself not to cry, retreating into an internal place well barricaded from me. What flashed through my mind in that moment was, *How hard would I have to spank her to make her cry*? It was a chilling thought, and immediately I knew this wasn't the solution, nor should it ever be the goal. I never spanked her again. We ended up resorting to a harness with a leash that we secured to our wrist. It proved effective. Passersby would glance at our canine solution, many giving us disapproving frowns. Others would pause to whisper, "*Where* did you get that? We need one!" The arrangement did not diminish her self-confidence in the slightest. On her fifth birthday, I was giving her some instructions (about what I no longer remember), and her response was, "Mama Ruth, I'm *five*—I know *everything*!"

One week, I was out of town at the same time Noelle's dads were too. This left Phyllis parenting alone during an intensely busy week of church duties. In addition to the usual pastoral care needs and church meetings, there was a wedding to prepare, a memorial service to officiate, and a sermon to be written for Sunday morning. Saturday evening arrived, and there was still no sermon written. Noelle simply wouldn't go to bed and stay there long enough for Phyllis to collect her thoughts and write. Now ten o'clock and thinking she had finally settled Noelle in for the night, Phyllis went into the kitchen to treat herself to a mug of warm milk and crackers before starting to write. She turned around to find Noelle in the doorway, opportunistically eyeing the crackers. Phyllis lost it. She hurled the box of crackers on the floor in front of Noelle and shouted, "Noelle, you have to go to bed *right now*!" Shocked by her normally patient mother's intense response, Noelle replied, "Mom, *that's* no way to tame your girl!" Out of the mouths of babes comes the very wisdom parents try to teach. Sometimes it gets used against us!

In parenting with Noelle's dads, the four of us worked out joint agreements that rejected the use of corporal punishment as "discipline." Instead, we agreed to use immediate, age-appropriate consequences for negative behavior coupled with opportunities for making amends whenever possible. It was sometimes challenging to come up with appropriate consequences in the moment. Jay remembered an incident when he realized a meaningful consequence was called for. "I knew I needed to think of something that had some teeth to it, but I was stumped. Suddenly, I heard myself saying, 'We were going to have Emma over this afternoon, but now we'll have to cancel your playdate for another time.'" He shook his head and added, "Of course that was a lie. There had been no scheduled playdate, but I was desperate." We laughed and assured him we understood completely.

When not involving safety, we tried to give Noelle as much autonomy in childhood as we reasonably could. She loved small spaces where she could create a den-like feel, even choosing to sleep on the floor of her closet with a sleeping bag, plenty of books, and some dolls for company. We chose to respect the unusual sleeping quarters she used for a while until spiders moved her out of them. We also encouraged her to keep a diary of her thoughts and feelings as her mother Phyllis had done in her own childhood. We assured Noelle we would read only what she chose to share with us (a promise we kept).

In addition to her private indoor hideaway, Noelle also enjoyed spending time tucked in the branches of our small backyard apple tree. We tried to honor our daughter's privacy and give her some sense of autonomy in a busy urban environment. We agreed to her wish not to be disturbed from her treetop hideaway for limited periods of time. We were keen to demonstrate our respect for her personhood so she would feel supported in her own self-respect. We extended these efforts to include her right to the privacy and safety of her own body. We taught her she always had a right to say, "No!" to unwanted touch of any kind from anyone and to tell us if anyone disrespected that right.

We decided that our tall privacy fence and our dog, always her loyal guardian, allowed us to relax our vigilance somewhat. However, one day with the help of branches that overhung the fence, she managed to drop down into our next-door neighbor's backyard when she saw he was sowing a wildflower garden and wanted to help him. We learned of this when he rang our bell, introduced himself, and handed us packets of wildflower seeds he had selected for her to plant in her own garden. This was the beginning of an "over the fence" friendship between them. He turned out to be a lovely gay man who won our trust.

A creative child of four creative parents, Noelle had high expectations of her two home environments. Having watched us at our hobbies, she knew our capabilities and expected us to share them. Her dads set the bar, surprising her on her return from a vacation with her moms with a complete bedroom redo. *The Little Mermaid* was one of her two favorite movies at the time, so they decided to take a week off and paint her bedroom accordingly. The underwater scene depicted each of the mermaid's friends swimming around the ocean "walls." The water reached almost to the ceiling where the waves broke, meeting the sky. Her dads explained the absence of the mermaid by telling Noelle, "The reason you don't see the mermaid is because, when you are in this room, *you* are the mermaid." Needless to say, she was delighted.

In the car on the way home from her fathers' house, Noelle said brightly, "Oh, Mama Ruth, in my home with you guys, you can paint my walls like *Spirit*" (her other favorite movie about a wild mustang). Deflecting her with something vaguely noncommittal, I went shopping for a throw with horses on it the next day. I hung it on one of her bedroom walls and unveiled it to her after school, hoping that would satisfy her. She replied, "That's nice, Mama Ruth. Now on the rest of the walls you can paint Spirit and the herd galloping. Don't forget the eagle flying over the mountains." I gave in, internally cursing Jay and Ched. I must admit though, it was a mural I am proud of.

Noelle herself was very artistic as a child, always busy making something in her room. We joked that her bedroom was proof of the chaos theory of the universe. I learned to quit saying, as I opened the door, "Yikes! What a mess this is!" I switched to saying, "Wow! You've really been busy being creative. Show me what you're working on." With great delight, she invariably would. Afterward, we would clean up together, though it was never long before the next creative mess.

In 2005, we made the difficult decision to move back to Minnesota. This gave Phyllis time to spend with her recently widowed mother and offered us the opportunity to eventually purchase an affordable home. For Noelle, claiming home in Minnesota without the roots Phyllis and I had took time. Trips back to see her dads kept up her connection with them but continually reminded her of the home she missed.

Noelle attended a middle school that offered a support group for children with gay and lesbian parents. At the staff's urging, Noelle attended a couple of meetings and then dropped out of the group. When asked why, Noelle replied, "Those kids are all embarrassed about having gay and lesbian parents. I'm not. Why should I join a group who are ashamed of their parents?" As the school continued its efforts to stand in solidarity with LGBT people, it announced that it would observe a "Day of Silence." Noelle thought that was absurd because, in her view, silence was a primary means of suppression of LGBT people and their history. She chose instead to wear her T-shirt with the slogan "SILENCE = DEATH" on it and refused to comply with spending the day in silence. This resulted in her being called to the principal's office. There she explained that discussion—not silence—was needed, because too many people were not at all familiar with the issues that contributed to LGBT invisibility. She pointed out that silence imposed by an inhospitable society was one of them. The staff listened and let her go without a reprimand.

Fortunately, one of Noelle's teachers had lived in San Francisco and understood some of the cultural clash that was taking place. She also recognized that Noelle was unhappily struggling to bridge two worlds. Her wisdom and understanding were helpful in Noelle's adjustment. A positive outcome to Noelle's open resistance to silence that day in school was that a boy in her class confided to her that his father was transitioning to a transgender woman. Before Noelle's arrival at his school, the boy had not felt he could tell anyone of this or invite any friend to his home. Noelle became a key support to him that year, going home with him after school several times.

It was a period in her life that continued to be challenging for her as well as for her parents. We knew we had a child with a mind of her own when she came home and reported that a classmate had asked her about her two moms. "You have a stepmom and a mom?" the girl had asked. "No," replied Noelle. "I have two moms." "You mean you have a godmom and a mom?" returned the child. "No, just two moms," Noelle repeated. "I don't get it," the girl replied. Playfully picking up a rubber band, Noelle stretched it out sideways before her classmate's eyes and replied, "*Expaaand* your mind, Melissa. I'm from San Francisco; expand your mind."

As Noelle has grown up, we have seen how her strong will, her passionate nature, and her early childhood experiences in community have shaped her into a young adult with some exceptional (and challenging) qualities. Noelle looks back on her childhood in San Francisco as having instilled in her a resilient spirit, a commitment to justice, and a high comfort level with difference. She rarely misses an opportunity to stand up and speak out when she perceives an injustice.

A mother now herself, Noelle says she wants to pass along these values to her son as well as the importance of learning from mistakes and making amends. "The amends was my favorite part as a kid, because it meant I could start over and change course. They could even be fun sometimes. But I am *never* walking Ciel with a leash!" she added firmly. "That's because you can keep up with him," I replied. However, after two episodes of Ciel staging a breakout and easily outstripping Grandma, Noelle agreed to the purchase of a backpack in the shape of a bear that had an attached leash. Tossing it to me, she said, "Tell him you're keeping the bear from getting lost!" I am glad to report that Ciel enjoys his bear, and boy, do I need that leash even more now!

Today we are a resource-rich society when it comes to parental guidance. Many in our parents' generation had to skip their childhood in order to work on behalf of their families. Many of our recent immigrants have to work multiple jobs to maintain basic economic stability. That exacts a steep price on the health and well-being of income earners and their children. My mother's background reflects some of this same struggle for economic stability. Her father died suddenly when she was only four years old and her sister was just three. At ten years of age, her brother became "the man of the family," who worked long hours after school while their mother cobbled together several small jobs, eventually opening up her home to boarders. In high school, my mother worked two jobs playing piano for silent movies and for a dance studio. Because of these difficult early years, doing things just for fun was simply not in her nurture. Fortunately, in marrying my father, she was grafted into another family that offered more stability, as well as nurture laced with fun.

My mother used to say to me, "I'll take the blame when my oldest girls lay it on me, but not from you and your brother. Thank heavens I got Dr. Spock's book in time for you two. I made up for all the hugs Miriam and Naomi were denied because my own doctor said holding them when they cried would spoil them. I doubled them up on you younger two." She then added, "And you know what you did when you grew up and came home for visits?" "No, what?" I asked. "You always hugged your dad and me and then taught your sisters to hug as well. We all hug now." "So those double hugs you gave me eventually paid off," I replied. "I guess they did," she answered with a smile.

Despite (and perhaps because of) the sorrows and challenges of her childhood, my mother had developed resilience. But her resilience had come at a price in her parenting. Her two younger children had an easier childhood than her two older ones, as she became more secure with the influence of a gentle partner. It is important to look at the power dynamics in our first families and take stock of how we may be perpetuating our caregivers' mistakes with us on our own children. No one is perfect, nor are we well trained for the most important job any parent/caregiver will ever have. Our parents' best may still not have been good enough, just as our best may fall similarly short.

With the benefit of hindsight, we know we are all in need of forgiveness and the possibility of changing course. It's no accident that grandparents tend to be better at "grandparenting" than they were at parenting. With experience comes wisdom. However, it is deeply ironic that while youth could use more wisdom for parenting, grandparents could use more energy for grandparenting. It makes one wonder if the stars ever truly align. I guess we just need each other.

Mapping and Blessing Our Homes

What we need from our homes and how we live in them changes over time as our family configurations change. But some things remain constant. We want a place where we get to be who we are and where we like who we are becoming with those who share our lives.

Establishing or redefining home often represents some kind of life transition such as geographical relocation, entering into a new relationship, staying in the home after a relationship breakup, the death of a family member, or becoming a blended family through the merger of homes. Whatever the reason, we must thoughtfully consider what we need from our home in times of transition.

It can be useful to initiate a new home or a new experience of a current home through a simple ritual of home blessing. This can take place privately among the family members who are (or will be) living in the home together, or it can stretch beyond to include families of the heart and others whom you name as part of your chosen community. Participants in such a ritual should be those who stand ready to support the occupants of the home during their time of transition.

Before having a blessing for a home, it is helpful to first map out how you wish to use your new home or repurpose the use of an old home. Start by identifying where the hearth/heart of your home is. How you intend to live there will set the tone for how you negotiate the use of all the other spaces in the home. This is because what you are really negotiating is how to be a family together. Establishing the heart of your home is even more important if you live alone, because sometimes it's all you can do to just come home and collapse at the end of the day. Your hearth grounds you in how you want to live. It holds you in your home's embrace.

During our time in San Francisco, we became good friends with a family who had purchased a lovely home up in the hills overlooking the city. Their home provided a stunning view of both the city and the Bay Bridge. While the Golden Gate Bridge draws tourists during the day, the Bay Bridge comes alive at night. Spanning from the city's heart across to Treasure Island, this beautiful suspension bridge glows as a necklace of lights reflected over dark waters.

One evening, we attended a fundraising event with Susan and Peter. We left their daughter and ours at their home in the capable hands of a gay couple we both knew who offered to provide childcare. In their day job, Rand and Jonathan staged homes that were for sale. When we stopped to pick up our sleeping daughter afterward, we chatted with Rand and Jonathan while waiting for Susan and Peter to come home.

Sitting in our friends' living room, we noticed that the arrangement of the room forced the occupants to choose between the hearth and the view, undercutting both and lending an unfinished quality to it. We also knew that high-intensity professional lives, parenting, and health concerns had used up their energy for fully making this house their home. As we all talked about what a beautiful living room it could be, we fantasized how we would arrange it to maximize both the fireplace hearth and the view. Suddenly overcome with mischief, the three of us came up with a plan for a redo of the room and began actually rearranging it (with Phyllis looking on in disapproval of our cheekiness).

We placed their beautiful Pakistani rug and their couch at a diagonal so the couch provided cozy seating facing the glass walls that converged in the view, while also opening up a view to the hearth that was built into a corner of the room. The two easy chairs we placed opposite the couch where they could pivot at will for the view or the hearth. We then moved the piano to create a musical tableau that did not dominate the room but invited one to sit down and play if so inclined. We utilized the existing works of art, which were both lovely and deeply meaningful, suggesting a couple of relocations for greater effect. However, we had the good sense to refrain from inflicting unsanctioned nail holes in the wall.

Then we sat down in the "new" living room and, like guilty children, waited for Peter and Susan to come home. When we heard their key in the lock, I met them at the door to warn them there was a surprise awaiting them. With one glance at my face, Susan exclaimed, "Oh, I think I *know* what this is. Show me!" Fortunately, both Susan and Peter chorused their hearty approval of the new arrangement and kept it for the remainder of their years in that house. In fact, in 2008, we had the pleasure of returning to San Francisco to marry yet again, grateful for our friends' offer of their home as our wedding venue. It became yet another special memory. This time the legality of our marriage held!

When we thoughtfully consider the heart of our home, we are doing what every business or spiritual community does. We are determining our "mission statement" based on what is most important to us and what best describes us. In the context of home living, it is what we wish for ourselves and for those who experience our home with us. In essence, your mission statement embodies the spirit of your home living.

We offer the following questions to help you create your mission statement and plan how you wish to live in your home. As you walk through each room, ask yourselves:

- What will be the designated purpose of this particular room?
- What activities and experiences do we hope will take place in our home?
- How will its furnishings serve these experiences?
- What space could be designated for quiet activity or creative renewal?
- Where can children more freely play in the home?
- What environment do we want for rest, solitude, intimacy, and hospitality?
- What does each person living here need from this home?

If it's a home you have been living in, it's important for each member to identify what has been getting in the way of how you want to live in it and to brainstorm together new ways of living in it. Think about how to reconfigure the use of your home space to accommodate multiuse. Be willing to listen to, and share with others who live with you, what each of you needs in order to feel at home. Perfect solutions are not the goal. The goal is flexible accommodations to what is possible as well as desirable.

If the home has outside acreage or a yard, it can be equally helpful to walk the grounds, envisioning how garden spaces can become home spaces and how outside nature interfaces with inside nurture. Here are some outdoor issues to consider:

- Where will we sit with our morning coffee before leaving for work?
- What are the needs of the feathered or furry creatures that share our lives?
- Where might we plant a garden, park a sandbox, or create a patio?
- Where do we locate the hearth of our outdoor space?

Note that outdoors, sometimes it's a water feature such as a pond or a fountain that creates the outdoor "hearth" or focal point for gathering.

If you have no access to outdoor space connected to your home, you may wish to select sunlit areas inside where plants can thrive, or a water fountain can be placed, or a small meditation table may hold symbols special to you. In tight spaces, a memory wall can offer space for photos that connect you to your family lineage or honor the relationships formed by families of choice. The symbols of water, fire, earth, and wind can invite the power and beauty of nature into your home. When we intentionally draw upon the symbols and ties that nurture and sustain us, we give them permission to grow in significance and power.

It is important to identify what we need from our homes, including each room, as well as outdoor spaces. Identifying the activities and relationships we wish to support within and outside our homes helps us voice our intentions for them and bring them to fruition. Gathering friends and family members allows them to bless our intentions and become part of them. We all need cheerleaders for our well-being and happiness who can also become supports in times of crisis or struggle.

Here in Minneapolis, when our family expanded to include our grandson and his parents living with us, we needed to reconfigure our space to accommodate them. They took over the upper level of our one-and-a-half-story bungalow as their living quarters. Since usable space upstairs is smaller than downstairs, we converted our enclosed front porch to a playroom for our grandson so there could be a little more room on the upper level. We share common areas downstairs. Noelle and Evan are also continuing the tradition of bedroom murals with their son. In Ciel's room, "Pops" has created a sun that radiates from the round globe overhead, enhanced by carefully painted rays exploding from the globe's center. Ciel loves it. We're a little worried, though, because he has clearly been set up to use his crayons on walls.

However, "child-proofing" downstairs—is there truly such a thing?—has meant having to part with two of my stained glass lamps. I received my first warning when I came out of the kitchen to find that Ciel, then seventeen months old, had climbed up on top of the dining room table and was reaching for the chandelier, entranced by its beauty. He followed this up a few days later with pulling a stained glass lamp off a file cabinet, exclaiming sadly as it fell and broke, "Oh, ohhh!" I finally got the message. So for now, we have compromised beauty for security with two extra-tall baby gates and the banishment of the best lamps to the basement. Our living room ambience has dimmed. However, my workspace in the unfinished basement now has a much nicer atmosphere!

Negotiating the needs of our extended family outdoors resulted in converting an area behind our garden shed so Ciel and his parents could have their own patio and raised garden bed, important to cooks who love their herbs and salads. Two Adirondack chairs and a chaise lounge provide comfortable seating, while a sandbox under a shady dwarf maple tree gives Ciel something to engage him as the adults visit. This provides them their own space and privacy when we sit on our patio with friends. We can hear each other's laughter but not our conversations. And one day, our grandson can climb his own tree.

The Power of Ritual in Homing

While we have had a number of home blessing rituals over the years, the most memorable one occurred in San Francisco shortly after moving into the parsonage. We wanted anyone in our church community who would like to participate in a blessing of our home to stop by after coffee hour. Since our colleague Michael Hiller was presiding at the service the following Sunday, we asked him to announce this impromptu invitation after the service.

However, that Sunday, Michael surprised us by attaching the blessing ritual to the service itself. Before the closing blessing, he instructed everyone to recess from the church by following the cross and banner that would be carried around the block to the parsonage for our home blessing. The entire congregation gaily processed to our home. People on the city streets gazed in surprise at this unusual sight, a few of them tagging along out of curiosity. Our garden, our home, and our life within it were thoroughly blessed that day by people both known and unknown to us. The power of it was palpable to everyone who participated in it. We got far more than we asked for, literally and figuratively!

We share the following home blessing ritual as an aid to imagining what you might wish to include in your own home blessing. Just as we have chosen families of the heart in each locale we have lived, so we have also chosen to have a blessing for each of our homes. Moreover, we also had a blessing ritual when we came together as a family with our daughter's fathers and then again when our second California marriage was legally affirmed in Minnesota. We have joked that we feel like we have married one another multiple times, but since each has come with another blessing, we don't regret any of them. In fact, we take seriously that we are "blessed to become a blessing."

Whether it's a home blessing or a relationship blessing, we have found that rituals help establish a foundation for these important chapters of our lives. They have also drawn upon and helped create community at every stage in our life together. All of our blessing rituals have included the sharing of food afterward. The following home blessing ritual weaves strands from past home blessings up through our present home in Minneapolis that we share with our daughter, her partner, and their son. We offer it as an example as you shape your own ritual.

Our Home Blessing Ritual

Outside the front door or threshold to the home:

Blessing of Welcome (door key or open door as symbol)
Reading: An Irish Blessing

"God bless the corners of this house,
And be the lintel blest.
And bless the hearth and bless the board
And bless each place of rest.
And bless each door that opens wide
To strangers and to kin.

And bless each crystal windowpane
That lets the starlight in.
And bless the rooftree overhead
And every sturdy wall.
The peace of humanity, the peace of God,
The peace of love on all."

~ Author unknown

Home Mission Statement

After guests have stepped inside, the hosts speak their home's mission:

"May this living space become a loving place that provides refuge, hospitality, and creative renewal to all who dwell here and all who cross its threshold. May we expand our hearts as our family reconfigures and our friendship circles widen. Through every stage of life, may this house always be a *Home with Heart*."

~ Ruth Frost and Phyllis Zillhart

Common Living Spaces

LIVING ROOM: Blessing of the Hearth (or whatever serves as the heart of the home)

Words of Welcome from the Hosts: Ruth Frost and Phyllis Zillhart

"We gather together as family in community to bless this house and all who help make it a home by celebrating with us. When we speak from the heart, others listen from their hearts. By the light and warmth of this hearth, we tell the old stories and make new stories that comfort and heal, that inspire and teach, connecting us more deeply to one another and to the gift of life. We thank each of you for your role in our lives and for celebrating with us this day."

Response from the Community:

"May the light of this hearth reflect the spark that glows within us all. May this family be warmth to those who gather here. May we who are their community fold them in our embrace."

~ Ruth Frost, *Prayers of Blessing*

DINING AREA: Blessing of Hospitality (a loaf of bread as symbol)

"May this dining room be a place where all are welcome at the table, where bodies are nourished and hearts filled, where new friendships form and old friendships deepen, and where solitude brings peace and company gives joy. May the abundance shared at this table remind us of the needs to fill at other tables; may we taste eternity in giving and receiving."

~ Ruth Frost, *Prayers of Blessing*

KITCHEN: Blessing of the Seasoned Life (herbs and spices as symbols)

Reading:

"It is Saturday morning and we awaken to the promise of breakfast, made by Evan, Noelle's partner. Scents of curry and turmeric, tomatoes and coriander waft enticingly our way. Evan is making his specialty, his own spin on a Moroccan potato omelet. Sweet, savory, and hearty, it is both comfort food and exotic promise to Midwestern palates. We are waking to a dish that has been crafted with love and imagination and considerable skill when flipped in an oversized pan holding ten eggs and three potatoes together. The sauce, which is Evan's secret, is the crowning touch. The omelet arrives at our table, served by our other chef, Noelle, who is an expert in plating food transformed into art. Ah . . . does life get any better than this?"

~ Ruth Frost, *Journal Memories*

Prayer:

"We give thanks for food and drink to sustain our lives and make our hearts glad. We receive the love that calls us together and names us family, seasoning our lives with zest and strengthening us in our travels."

~ Ruth Frost, *Prayers of Blessing*

PERSONAL SPACES

BATHROOM: Blessing of Cleansing and Renewal (water as symbol)

Reading:

A paraphrase of Psalm 23, from Hebrew Scripture

"You, O God, are my shepherd.
You provide for my needs.
You let me rest in fields
of green grass.
You lead me to streams
of peaceful water.
You refresh my life."

Adapted from the 1995 Contemporary English Version

Prayer of Renewal:

"In the amniotic fluid of our mother's waters, we experienced our first home in this world, nurtured by those waters until we were called out of the deep and into the bright light of the sun and the cool soil of earth. We remember our primordial origins in the sea, womb of Mother Earth. As we bathe our bodies in warm water, we affirm God's welcome into the wide world of the human family. As we drink cool water, we give thanks for its life-sustaining power in our bodies made up mostly of water. As we stand under showers, may the rains of heaven mingle with the tears of earth and wash our eyes clear of sorrow, freeing us to open our hearts and envision again our common humanity. Let us remember and celebrate the gift of water that births us and sustains us and refreshes our souls."

~ Ruth Frost, *Prayers of Blessing*

BEDROOM: Blessing of Rest (a sprig of lavender as symbol)

Prayer for Peaceful Rest:

"Holy One, be our light in the darkness, and in your mercy, defend us from all perils and dangers of the night. Calm our sleepless worries and awaken us to gifts hidden in darkness: the stars that could not be seen unless folded into night, the stillness of birds resting, the rhythmic sound of breath rising and falling, the deep sleep that follows bodies given and received from the heart of love, the gift of dreams that come as greetings from worlds as yet unseen. In the darkness of the night, bring us rest and intimate connection with you and those we hold dear. Hold back fear and open us to awe. Bless us with the mystery of night and the illumination of dawn."

~ Ruth Frost, *Prayers of Blessing*

CHILD'S PLAYROOM: Blessing of Creative Play (a favorite toy as symbol)

Reading:

"As I open the door to the porch, the sun casts streams of light onto an architectural wonder. I smile as I look at the whimsical tower my daughter has created for her son to discover when he comes downstairs to enjoy what is now his playroom. She has stacked the three-foot tower using his books and blocks to form each level, creating something akin to an open-air parking ramp. Standing precariously on top of each other, a hodgepodge of toy cars and farm animals occupy each level. A stuffed troll grumpily sits at its base as though ready to collect parking fees. I poke my head in when I hear our grandson's giggles after he discovers this fantastical tower. For several seconds he examines it, transfixed by its wondrous sight. Then with arms raised and hands waving, he trots over to it and, in one exuberant swoop, brings it all tumbling down. It is demo day in the playroom, and he laughs delightedly, anticipating other towers to come. Later, he will build his own tower."

~ Ruth Frost, *Journal Memories*

Prayer of Thanksgiving for Wonder:

"We give thanks for the gift of creativity and a child's daily sense of wonder; may our children inspire us to play. Help us stretch our imaginations for creativity that renews us, delights our senses, and feeds joy."

~ Ruth Frost, *Prayers of Blessing*

OUTDOOR SPACES

PATIO: Blessing of Time Out of Time (two coffee mugs as symbols)

Reading:

"Early morning birdsong greets my rising. My partner has walked the dog and put on the coffee, hoping its aromatic flavors will entice her family to enter the day. The cat meows insistently, demanding his bowl first while the dog dances impatiently around him, nails eagerly clicking on the kitchen floor, waiting for hers to be filled. I dress and make our lunches for work and school. While others sleep, I grab two cups of coffee and whisper, 'Meet me on the patio.' We sit in the rising sun, sipping coffee, feeling like clandestine lovers. Even the dog has tactfully excused herself to go on squirrel patrol. We bask in the blessing of time out of time!"

~ Ruth Frost, *Prayers of Blessing*

Reading:

"I used to think that coffee breaks were trivial times, pleasant interruptions in the real work of the day. I see them now as times for reaching in and reaching out—moments of grounding in the still center of our souls and moments when we lean our fears and hopes on one another, resting places for God's journeying people."

~ Adapted from Gerhard Frost, *Seasons of a Lifetime*

GARDEN: Blessing of Growth (a plant or a ripe fruit as symbol)

Reading:

"Planting cherry tomato beds and bush beans with my little grandson, who is too young to talk much but old enough to sample the veg, I marvel at the prodigality of Mother Earth. Overhead, the aspens sway in the breeze, catching the sun's reflection in leaves that shine down on us silver trails of light. As I plant, my grandson overturns earth, occasionally tasting its richness. When I have declared our task finished, he carefully places his little blue truck in the garden bed as company for the plants, his own blessing for their growth. Later in the summer, we pick the cherry tomatoes and beans for our supper salads, taking time to sample the tomatoes as we pick. I bite each one in half and place the other half in his mouth. Like a baby bird, he waits open-mouthed, juice dripping down his chin, anticipating the next delicious moment. *'Mmmm . . . good,'* we both declare."

~ Ruth Frost, *Journal Memories*

CLOSING (at the back door or outside):

A Gaelic Blessing

Hosts:

"Deep Peace of the running wave to you.
Deep Peace of the flowing air to you."

Guests:

"Deep Peace of the quiet earth to you.
Deep Peace of the shining stars to you."

Hosts:

"Deep Peace of the gentle night to you.
Moon and Stars pour their healing light on you.
Deep Peace to you."

~ Author Unknown

Honoring a Home Legacy

Introduction

This is the story of a couple, Ruth and Don, who planned to retire and build a home on family-owned lake property in Northern Minnesota. What followed is a remarkable example of continuing a legacy that has benefited four generations of family and their friends. I visited with them on the deck of their beautiful log home overlooking the lake, where their property is adjacent to our own. Since my name is also Ruth, I am designated here as interviewer.

INTERVIEWER: This property has benefited four generations so far, and who knows how many more to come. Can you describe how this lake home came about and the living arrangements that have unfolded within it?

RUTH:: When Don and I were ready to retire, we wanted to build a home for ourselves on the back acreage of this property. The only structure on the land was the original cabin Uncle Jack had built when he bought the two and a half acres of land sixty years ago from his brother for two hundred and fifty dollars. Jack eventually sold the property to his older sister for the same price he paid. She eventually passed it on to her younger sister, my mother. So my siblings and I grew up enjoying this property together. Everyone eventually created their own families but continued to return to these beautiful north woods that had become special to all of us.

Originally, when we were thinking about retiring, I contacted my brother to sound him out on whether he thought it might be okay with everybody if we built our retirement home in the woods behind the original structure. His reply was, "I don't think anyone would have a problem with that. But why not tear down the old cabin and rebuild on the lakefront site so you get the benefit of the view? You just have to build something big enough for us to visit." And so it was agreed, and a partnership arrangement satisfactory to everyone was settled on.

INTERVIEWER: So how many families share it now?

RUTH: Through the years we have shared this site with seven families including two nieces on Don's side of the family.

DON: The plan was to build a log home whose two levels would each have beautiful views of the lake. We created two separate living spaces and independent access on both levels. We heard from family members that they would like the lower level to have reminders of the old cabin. So we used a similar open floor plan and saved some of the furnishings from the old cabin for the new build. We wanted to create a tie to the old place in a more comfortable environment.

RUTH: We kept the bookcase that reminds us of Aunt Esther, an easy chair we all loved, and the dining room table my dad made where we played games and had wonderful meals and conversations. We housed the books Mother collected from her years as a librarian on the lower level so they would be accessible to everyone. My siblings report that when they stay downstairs, they feel like they are still at home in the old cabin. When they come upstairs, they are visiting us in our home.

INTERVIEWER: This plan seems to be working out well.

DON: Yes, this has become a very successful arrangement for everyone. The property gets much better care with us living here year-round. This means vacation time for visiting family members doesn't get eaten up by property needs as it used to. With added lodging in the garage and the cabana down by the lakefront and your cabin next door, this has become the favorite place for family reunions as well as for family vacations.

INTERVIEWER: Speaking of reunions, you had one reunion that brought together your extended family and a niece you had never met who had been given up for adoption years ago. Was it a surprise for her to be re-united with a much larger family than she might have anticipated?

RUTH: We had all been in touch with her prior to her arrival, so that helped. But the reunion occurred before she met my sister—her birth mother—who is living in the UK and can't travel due to having multiple sclerosis. She was happy and a bit overwhelmed to discover the extent of her family and our welcome. We tried not to scare her too much!

INTERVIEWER: What's it been like to share this property with so many other relatives?

RUTH: Oh, I think it has drawn us all together more. We have reunions where everyone gathers, and of course each family comes up other times on their own. I know I've gotten to know all my nieces and nephews much better, as well as my cousins. It's kept me more current with my siblings too.

DON: As our nieces and nephews have grown up, their generation has had their own reunions up here. It's great to see what this lake property has come to mean to them.

INTERVIEWER: You never know what lives a place will hold. I know some of your family members have come here when they're going through tough times. Your hospitality has been a healing balm to many. I think of your sister Susan who came here after her chemo treatments in the midst of dealing with cancer. She found support and rest here.

RUTH: We try. We let people know they can come here with no preconceived plans and can do as much or as little as they want. They can have our company or their privacy—whatever they need. Most of the time, this place gives them what they need.

DON: We've had several people say how they sleep better here than anywhere else. I think it's the air.

INTERVIEWER: And the company they keep. I think of your sister, Don, who struggles with memory loss and her husband who is so steadfast in providing care in their home for her. Up here he doesn't have to feel alone in his care, and she finds refuge in a simpler life.

DON: Yes, it's interesting because she was never much of a nature lover. She's always preferred a busy city life. But since her illness, she enjoys the quieter pace of the North Country. She sits on the deck here—which is really the "hearth" of our home in the summer—and takes in the sound of waves lapping and the call of the loons and the quiet peace of this place. No one is testing her memory or asking her for something she can't give. We're in the moment together.

INTERVIEWER: This is a healing place.

RUTH: Yes, that's true.

INTERVIEWER: Do you see yourselves ever leaving this place?

DON: Absolutely not!

RUTH: I never say "absolutely" because you never know how your circumstances can change. But this is a very special place.

INTERVIEWER: What avenues have you found for enjoying friends up here?

RUTH: Well, certainly our study group. The first book we read was the Koran because we wanted to be better schooled in Islam. And then we read *The Road to Character,* followed by *Great Speeches.* More recently we read *The Book of Joy* with Desmond Tutu and the Dalai Lama. Another group we're both in started with reading a book called *The Monk and the Philosopher.* Eventually, we named ourselves "The MONK Group," "MONK" becoming our tongue-in-cheek acronym for "Mindful of Not Knowing."

INTERVIEWER: Sounds very enlightened!

RUTH: We've enjoyed learning more about Buddhism. Tonight we are meeting to talk about St. Augustine. So we're pretty eclectic in our learning.

DON: When we first moved here, we thought we might be isolated and lonely. So we joined an early morning walking group that walks daily. Ruth has a weaving group, and I joined the curling club. I also play chess once a week. So I guess we missed out on being hermits! (laughter)

INTERVIEWER: What does living on the lake give you spiritually?

DON: Well, to start with, it gives us the lake. Do you know what dharma is?

INTERVIEWER: Only vaguely. Tell me more.

DON: It's the nature of things just as they are. From a Christian viewpoint, you might think of it as God's creation, but because it's Buddhist, there is no God. Another word for it is "suchness." It is what is. So what it means to me—especially here on this little hearth spot—is dwelling in suchness or dharma. Living here by the lake is peaceful.

INTERVIEWER: I know you have gone through a lot of family losses. Does this place help in times of loss?

DON: Certainly! It gives me comfort. And I think it gives the rest of the crowd using this place comfort. At least I hope it does.

RUTH: Kabekona Lake is extremely special to us. Growing up, my family moved a lot. To borrow a phrase from indigenous Native American peoples, this was our "center of the earth" throughout all that moving. This is where we had time to relax and enjoy being a family. Now my parents are buried in the little country cemetery not far from here.

INTERVIEWER: In addition to comfort, this place seems to foster creativity. Your dad was always making things, and your mother would team with him. I remember the year your dad killed a deer with a bow and arrows he'd made. In addition to using its meat, he made a fireplace bellows from its hide, and your mom tooled a wildlife scene in the leather. Then we received it as a Christmas present from your family. That bellows still hangs over the hearth in our cabin next door where it is a treasured tool of great beauty.

RUTH: Yes, this is an environment that encourages people to relax with a creative project or curl up with a good book or take time for leisurely conversation.

INTERVIEWER: My father used to get up at dawn to write poetry down on the dock as he watched the sun rise. In fact, our little cabin was built from the royalties my dad saved from his books. I think of him with gratitude as I work on my own writing up here. I have fond memories of going for walks in the woods as a family, and my mother periodically stopping us with, "Shhh, let's listen to the silence." We would all freeze in our tracks and listen to the sounds of the woods and the rustling of its wildlife—sounds human chatter would scare away.

RUTH: And I remember my parents making us go outside after dark to look up at the stars. City dwellers can't know how bright the night sky is, nor can they know the beauty of the aurora borealis casting green and gold and purple hues over the night waters.

DON: One day, on a very short walk, I saw four deer, a grouse, two turkeys, and a beaver. How many places can that happen to you on a single walk?

INTERVIEWER: That's what makes this place special. Most of the properties around here are weekend getaways that stand empty otherwise. This place is far from empty. In addition to the many families using it, it has become a connection to the previous generations. Their presence is palpable up here. While I am very attached to our home in the city, this place has a spiritual quality to it that is special. In addition to bonding with nature, Phyllis and I use time up here for relational renewal. We read to each other and have long conversations by the fire. I find balance up here, and we find each other again in that renewal.

DON: There is an element of use to a house that makes it a home. You know how a new pair of shoes becomes comfortable over time? It's that way with a house after long-term use.

INTERVIEWER: Yes, and when you live in a house that has been in a family through generations, there is a gifted quality to that house—it gives itself all over again to another generation, and you inherit that gift from the previous generation. It's like planting a tree as a sapling. It's so small in your hands when you plant it. You plant it for a future you cannot fully envision, but in planting, you declare your faith in that future and the generations that will follow you. You trust its yield, even though you have only the glimpse of your lifetime.

DON: That's suchness.

RUTH: And speaking of suchness, I've made a peach pie. Anyone want some?

INTERVIEWER: Ahhh . . . suchness with muchness!

Healing Painful Associations with Home

Sometimes painful events have occurred in our homes that leave an indelible imprint upon those who continue to live in them. It may be a single occurrence such as a home break-in or a family member's death. It may be a pattern of harmful incidents such as those of an ex-partner who has left a legacy of domestic abuse. Whatever type of event, the result may create an unavoidable association with the home that scars the hearts and minds of those who may have no other option but to continue living there. The pain associated with such events can be continuously triggered simply by ongoing residence in the home. In such instances, the old adage "Time heals all wounds" merely mocks the survivor.

Before going any further, let me first acknowledge that the situation I address in this chapter, while very serious, is different from those that arise from living in dangerous neighborhoods where gangs, drug dealing, and gun violence are a constant threat. I don't know how anyone can sustain living in a state of "red alert" all the time. And yet there are those that have to. While I have seen the toll that homelessness takes on the physical and mental health of people, I cannot fathom the stress of living in a neighborhood that has become a virtual war zone where the possibility of safety no longer exists inside or outside the home. Honesty compels me to admit that I can offer little of value to those who are trapped in those living conditions.

If our homes are to be what they were intended—places of peace and refuge in time of need—it can truly be said that our homes as well as their occupants have been violated when violence occurs in them. This is dangerous territory, and certainly those who have experienced trauma in their homes should not try to address it without skilled support. A small group of people, such as a trauma therapist working in concert with a wise spiritual guide and a few trusted friends or family members, can lend their support when the survivor's emotional resources are temporarily disabled. In times of great stress, sometimes such a healing "team" can lend strength to the survivor until a path of eventual self-healing may be found.

While there are no quick fixes for deep healing, daily meditation or prayerful communion with Spirit can offer rest for the soul. In our spiritual practice as pastors and later as hospice chaplains, both Phyllis and I have employed home rituals as a means of reframing and reclaiming physical home space that has been violated. We see ritual as a fitting accompaniment to other avenues for healing from traumatic events or painful associations. Cleansing physical home space and strengthening home security (spiritually and physically) within the nexus of loving community can restore a measure of comfort and safety to those who continue to reside in potentially toxic environments. The goal is to mitigate the negative association's harmful effects by creating life-affirming experiences (coupled with community support) that have the power to initiate new healing associations. What follows provides an example of how this may be useful.

Sarah's Story

I met Sarah while co-facilitating a group that was discussing life transitions and their effects on "homing." Some of the group members attended with a friend; others made friends while sharing their various life stages and stories. Sarah was an interested but quieter member of the group. In my introduction, I said the last of our six sessions would end with a blessing ritual of someone's home chosen by lottery from the names submitted. At the next-to-last session, we talked about the lottery and someone said, "I think we should just let Sarah have a blessing if she wants it." This was a curious development because Sarah hadn't said anything in our time together as a group that suggested she was seeking one. But Sarah readily accepted this offer when it became apparent that the group was happy to give her that option.

I later learned in a separate exchange with Sarah that she had a story to tell. She was a single parent with an adult son who had gotten into drug use and the troubles that went with it. Having lost his housing, her son Jason had been staying temporarily with her, bunking on the couch in the basement family room with his dog, Buddy. Night after night, he would come home late after partying with his friends. Lying awake worrying, Sarah could never fall asleep fully until he arrived home safely.

One night, after Jason had come home, and Sarah had finally fallen asleep, she was wakened by Buddy pawing her. Glancing at the clock, she saw it was three in the morning. She was tempted to roll over and go back to sleep, but something about Buddy's intensity sounded a warning. She got up and followed Buddy, who led her to the basement. Snapping on the light at the head of the stairs, she saw her son lying motionless on the cement floor at the base of the steps. Her heart pounding, she raced down the steps and found him unconscious, his pupils dilated. Immediately, Sarah dialed 911 for emergency help. She then administered CPR until the medics arrived to take over and rushed him to the hospital.

Thankfully, Jason lived and eventually went into a rehabilitation program, staying in transitional housing until he had fully completed treatment. But while Jason was gone and working on sobriety, Sarah became stuck in the nightmarish scenario of finding her son on the floor of her laundry room. She said, "Every time I go downstairs to do laundry, I am back in that scene of finding my son and believing I had lost him forever. I can't shake the association." She went on to say she was taking care of Jason's dog while he was gone. She added that she would ask her next-door neighbor to keep Buddy at her house the day of the blessing, as he could be rambunctiously friendly, and she didn't want to have to worry about how he would behave among so many people he didn't know.

Sarah said she would prefer to invite the group to the blessing without telling them beforehand why she wanted one. I suggested we save the basement as the last space to be blessed inside the house. She could tell her story while we were gathered around the spot where she had found her son. We would then leave the dark basement, ending with a blessing of the garden, the symbol of light and new life. Sarah readily agreed to this plan.

Meanwhile, the group decided we should have potluck breakfast first, followed by the blessing. The day of the blessing, group members arrived in high spirits eager to share breakfast and experience the blessing ritual. In consultation with Sarah, I had selected some readings for each room's blessing and distributed them among the group to read at each appointed place. Sarah had chosen symbols of significance for each room. The mood throughout was respectfully friendly and readily participative. When it was time to go downstairs to the basement, I instructed the group to descend the dimly lit stairway safely and gather in a circle at the base of the stairs where Sarah had a story she would tell them. A hush swiftly descended over them, and they quietly complied.

Standing in our circle at the base of the steps where Sarah had discovered Jason, Sarah lit a single candle and told her story with the light of its small flame flickering gently across her expressive face. When she was finished, after a moment of silence, I invited her to enter our circle to receive spontaneous blessings from group members. Sarah stepped in, and the group drew instinctively closer. The atmosphere of high spirits had changed, and in its place, a quiet power settled over us and among us. One by one, each member of the group took turns stepping inside the circle with Sarah. Gently placing a hand on her shoulder, they graced her with their blessing. When we were finished, we ascended out of the darkness into the bright sunshine of the backyard garden.

There, his nose pressed close against the fence mesh, was Buddy, softly whining. I turned to Sarah and said, "Given his role in this, I think he deserves to join us for this part. What do you think?" She immediately agreed, and Buddy joined our circle, sitting quietly in our midst for the last blessing of the garden and all its creatures, particularly the one with the wagging tail.

Afterward, people lingered, enjoying the bond that comes with participating in something that was far more important than they had expected, and knowing that they had each had a part in awakening Sarah from her nightmare. I later received a very gracious note of thanks from Sarah stating how beautiful the experience had been and how much it had meant to her. "My house is now my home again."

Overcoming Clutter with Sacred Giving

Like many, I have become hooked on reality TV home makeover and fixer-upper shows. I think part of their popularity is that they provide a window into how people live (or want to live) in their homes. It's no secret that a key obstacle to joyful home living is a home overwhelmed by clutter. Such shows often end with a grand reveal of the before and after pictures of a home newly redesigned and displaying no trace of clutter. The trouble is, clutter that is swept away by "clutter genies" while the home's occupants are absent is likely to get recreated after their return, especially if the issues underlying clutter remain unaddressed. It's important to look at those issues. When they are addressed without judgment, people can hear without shame. Change then becomes not merely possible but truly liberating.

In a society driven by consumerism, status and self-worth get reflected in the acquisition of goods. If we have unmet emotional needs, it's tempting to seek things that can quickly distract us from low spirits, temporarily filling the emptiness. With the ease of online shopping, we get instant gratification. But instead of enriching us, acquisitions obtained impulsively end up cluttering our home environments, fraying family relationships, and wreaking havoc with family budgets. Most importantly, they mask our true yearnings. Acquisition becomes the false solution for lives that are out of balance. It feeds on feelings of shame, loss, insecurity, anxiety, or depression by temporarily buying them off. The "quick fix" of today becomes the clutter of tomorrow.

Clutter doesn't have to be worthless to be clutter. Homes can be cluttered by expensive goods as easily as they are by cheap goods. When possessions of any kind overwhelm our physical spaces, they choke off our desire to freely open our homes and hearts to relationships that could support and nurture us. Instead of being places that offer refuge and hospitality, homes become containers of chaos and anxiety, which are then shrouded in secrecy and shame, sealed by isolation.

Children are seriously affected by clutter when they are not given the opportunity to care for and put away their clothes and toys in designated places. I was once in a home that was so cluttered that a three-year-old child living there had nowhere to put her beloved books. I watched her carefully line up each of her books in the hallway, returning again to put them back when the adults would walk by the congested area and inadvertently kick them aside in passing. Eventually, with nowhere to put their possessions, children may conclude they have neither agency nor responsibility for their things and that they and their possessions are without value. Playthings need a home within the home where they can be easily found and appreciated like old friends. If they have no place to belong, neither do the children who love them. This further deprives children of a home environment that is welcoming of playmates and the fertile field of imagination. Worse, it can put children at risk if they resort to playing unattended in public spaces in order to delay going home to an environment that overwhelms them and makes them feel lost.

My partner, Phyllis, was one of those children who avoided home as much as she could. She was simply overwhelmed by the physical environment, her father's retreat into alcohol, and the inability to find her own place in that home. She recalls how important her small town church was to her when she was a young teenager. "The church became my escape from our chaotic, cluttered family home. My pastor had been inside our house when he made his visitation calls so he knew of its condition, but he never spoke of it. What he did do was quite extraordinary. He gave me a key to the church with permission to use it anytime I chose. So I used that key to seek refuge in the sanctuary, where I could sit in the dark and play the piano by the light of the 'eternal flame' on the altar. That key provided many hours of solace in a safe and peaceful environment where I could feel the presence of God's love. I had been given a place of belonging in God's house." As time passed, the congregation gave Phyllis a sphere in which her musical gifts and budding leadership skills could thrive and be of service within the community. In the process, she found her home and her calling to ministry.

Acquisition sometimes grows out of a family history of economic insecurity and deprivation. This can result in the inability to part with anything, even if it has outlived its usefulness. The message ingrained is: "Everything must be kept because everything can be lost." This is exemplified by the Great Depression following World War I. Someone inheriting this legacy may walk the alleys, compulsively picking up what others have tossed out because their family once had to "make do" during a time of hardship that appeared to have no end in sight. It doesn't help that our consumer-based society makes cheap goods designed for intentional obsolescence to keep people repetitively needing them. This is hard on the environment as well as invasive to our homes.

Anyone who is working on reducing ongoing problems with clutter may benefit from using outside resources for help. Organizational consultants can assist in creating systems to organize, categorize, and prioritize our possessions. Financial advisors can offer advice regarding which records to throw out and which to keep in hard copy or electronic files.

Therapeutic support offers a path to lasting change by providing tools for managing the anxiety, depression, and even grief that may underlie cluttered environments. Today, we are fortunate to have resources available online as well.

The good news is that we can challenge our own beliefs about ourselves that have been internalized by shame. By changing patterns of thinking, we can change the way we feel and act. I offer one approach to meaningful change from my years working in a treatment setting that proved effective in creating personal transformation. While not related directly to the problem of clutter, it demonstrates the possibility of enacting lasting change through group support and the use of a simple exercise.

Our clients seeking treatment for chemical dependency worked very hard on barriers to sobriety. Among those barriers were "shame messages" clients had received in their formative years that shaped their core sense of self and affected their ability to form stable relationships in adulthood. Clients did the bulk of their therapeutic work in family-sized groups that were facilitated by experienced therapists and counselors, most of them personally in recovery as well. Clients were encouraged to pay close attention to shame messages internalized from family and school as well as from religious and social institutions. They were asked to make a list of their shame messages. Clients never had any difficulty coming up with that list. In fact, we had to ask them to prioritize their top ten shame messages.

With the help of the client therapy group, each person's list of shame messages was converted to worth-based affirmations. So, for example, the hateful shame message, "You're nothing but a faggot and a drunk," was transformed into "I am a proud gay man who is sober today." The shame message, "You are eternally condemned because God hates gays," became "I am unconditionally loved because God created me just as I am." After working on their lists, clients then brought their list of affirmations to our daily Community Meeting of clients and staff. In Community Meeting, everyone gathered in a circle, linked arm in arm. As each client shared aloud one of their affirmations, the group would echo it back. For example, the echo response to "I am a proud gay man who is sober today" became "Yes! You *are* a proud gay man who is sober today."

In the first week of treatment, newcomers read their freshly minted affirmations in soft, tremulous voices, often with lowered heads, speaking to the floor. But by the time they were ready to leave residential treatment for outpatient services, they were smiling confidently and speaking by heart their now internalized affirmations with conviction and pride. Their heads uplifted, each made full eye contact with their loudly enthusiastic chorus as it shouted back their affirmations in ringing tones. What had become embedded as a shaming slur was recast to become an even stronger affirmation of value. These affirmations became a daily shared exercise in building a healthy core of self-love. Our recovering clients became living proof that shame messages can indeed be overcome when converted to worth-based messages with the help of caring community.

With respect to the issue of clutter, some of the beliefs we tell ourselves may be intergenerational in their origins. By identifying their origins, we can externalize them and begin to separate ourselves from them. This begins the process of compassionate understanding of self and others, clearing a path for mindful living. "When you're mindful, you carefully observe your thoughts and feelings without judging them as good or bad . . . mindfulness means living in the moment and awakening to your current experience, rather than dwelling on the past or anticipating the future." [13] Because rumination and worry contribute to depression, mindfulness practice helps reduce anxiety. As mindfulness helps us declutter our minds of old beliefs, it also helps us declutter our physical space of old stuff.

We let go of old beliefs by transforming them into new beliefs that invite positive change into our lives. The following beliefs people have internalized are examples of this. "I shouldn't throw this because that would be wasteful, and one day it might become useful" can be recast as "By giving this away, I am reclaiming this space to share with people I love." The old belief that says, "If I have to see my stuff as junk, I'm afraid I'll feel like junk," can become "I am letting go of things I no longer need because I am good enough without all this stuff." The self-abnegating message "I don't deserve a nice house" becomes "I deserve to have a home I love and a place where the people I love can feel at home."

In her book *Spark Joy,* Japanese author Marie Kondo helps people divest of clutter by a positive approach that takes into account whether each item being considered "sparks joy." Using prescribed categories, people work their way through each level of attachment, getting practice letting go. In the process, they learn how to reshape their environment to maximize freedom. Without judgment, hers is an inspirational approach to decluttering that energizes her clients each step of the way through the practice of gratitude. She provides her readers with helpful strategies for valuing and organizing what remains. Her methods are noteworthy for their staying power.

Yet another approach to changing one's relationship to possessions is to learn sacred giving and receiving as practiced by Native American nations. In our early years together, Phyllis and I were blessed to have a friend who was a member of the Anishinaabe nation. Carole shared from her culture the practice of holding a giveaway. "Unlike a garage sale, a giveaway is not for the purpose of making some money by getting rid of possessions. It's to freely give to the community and to honor the Creator and our Mother Earth, through whom all gifts come."

Giveaways can accompany such important gatherings as powwows, weddings, and naming ceremonies. They are also a way of remembering and honoring someone who has died. In the giveaway, the community comes together to give thanks. The family hosting the giveaway dances and then lays out their gifts on a large blanket. Then, allowing the Spirit to guide them, everyone is invited to come and quietly take one thing. In his article "Sacred Giving, Sacred Receiving," Joseph Bruchac talks about how the order of the recipients respects the community: elders are first, followed by veterans, women, little children, older children, and then men. Bruchac states that strengthening community is ". . . a gifting more akin to prayer than to self-aggrandizement and acquisition." [14]

If majority culture could learn from this practice, it would not only change our relationship to our possessions, but it could truly change the way we live. It would shift our focus from acquisition to the freedom of simplicity with mindful appreciation for quality. It would encourage greater connection to the people behind the gift or the purchase, whether they are still in this world or have passed on. Finally, it would free us for the renewal of relationships and for gifting others through gratitude. Carole left this world some time ago, but the gift she left behind is the power of the giveaway.

Our family has been richly blessed by a large number of extended family members. Our little grandson has three generations of relatives who generously provide him with everything they think he should have, sometimes in loving excess of what he needs. As he outgrows clothing and toys that have had no time to wear out, his parents delight in passing this generosity along. A friend of our daughter who has fewer resources is receiving what she needs, together with an organization that assists low-income single moms. It is a joy to pack up our grandson's shoes and outfits, imagining the many other little feet that will run around in them exploring their surroundings.

As we simplify our living and our possessions, we get clarity about how we want to live, and our beliefs about ourselves start to change. We become free to ask: "Are we at home in our own homes?" "Has this living space become a loving place?" "What is it that grounds us in purposeful, authentic living?" "What do we want people to experience in our home?" The answers to these questions will direct how we live.

Using Symbols to Hold Memories

Sometimes, the core issue that crowds a home is the aftermath of grief following the deaths of family members. With their passing, we are left with the previous generation's treasures. These increased, unlooked-for acquisitions, coupled with a misguided sense of loyalty to our loved ones' stuff, can quickly overburden our homes and take control of our psychic space as well as our physical space.

We fear that if we let go of the things that were important to our loved ones, we are being disloyal to them and disrespecting our relationship with them. We think we have to care about everything they cared about. Gradually, we find ourselves living with too many things vying for space we really don't have in our homes. What begins as gift becomes obligation to the past. We would do well to remember that when it comes time to leave this world, we all travel in the lightness of being. Perhaps we can benefit from practicing this more in our current life.

Recently, one of our friends was trying to deal with having inherited too many things from her deceased mother, whom she loved dearly. Her mother was a pianist and a music teacher to children. Her mother's piano, so symbolic of her service to others, sat cherished but mostly untouched in the small dining room it had taken over. Sitting silently in her daughter's home for several years, the piano ceased to sing her mother's musical celebration of life. Lynn loved what the piano stood for and the memories of her mother it evoked, but she reluctantly realized she had no time for the piano. She decided to honor her mother's legacy by giving the piano to Keys for Kids, a charitable organization that gave children who would not otherwise have access to a piano or music lessons the opportunity to have both. Not only did Lynn give away the piano, she also paid to have it moved so the organization did not bear that expense. In so doing, she honored her mother's legacy in full and gave it new purpose.

When we have difficulty letting go of things, symbols have the power to both represent and embody what we think we could lose. They invoke deeper truths and connect us with those who have gone before us. Symbols also aid us in discerning what to keep and how much to let go. Because they hold meaning, they can carry a heavy load. After Lynn gave away her mother's piano, the symbol Lynn chose to keep as a reminder of her mother's life in music was her metronome. Her mother had used it to help her students hear the music's heartbeat as they played.

Later, as her "family of the heart" gathered for dinner one evening, Lynn remarked that her "giveaway" had the unexpected result of liberating an overcrowded room for its original use: namely, hospitality around food and friendship. And we, who were the recipients of that hospitality, felt the spirit of "Mother June" honoring us in blessing.

Years ago when Phyllis was about to begin college several hours away from her hometown, her father volunteered to drive her, as she had no car. En route, he was ill at ease and very quiet, having never gone beyond eighth grade. He was disappointed that his daughter hadn't taken his advice and enrolled in technical school to become a dental assistant because, as he explained, "You would always have a job since people will always need their teeth cleaned." He was further bewildered that her intended majors were classical Greek coupled with religious studies. Nevertheless, he wanted to see his daughter safely to her destination. He knew he was taking her into a world he had never known and where he could not follow. Reaching her dormitory at last, it was time to say goodbye. He hesitated, knowing this was an important moment, but at a loss as to what to say. Clearing his throat, he reached deep into the pocket of his overalls and pulled out a pair of pliers. "Here, Phyl," he said, "take these. You never know when you might need them." She thanked him and then they parted.

The pliers, which had once belonged to Phyllis's grandfather before her father received them, hold a place of honor in our home. They take up very little space but are highly valued. They signify the essence of a man who worked hard manual labor all his life and who was rooted in the farming community of Southwestern Minnesota. In giving that much-used and highly practical tool to his daughter, her father tried to equip her for life in the way he knew. In so doing, he passed on part of himself. What it symbolizes is far more than its worth. But it has great meaning and power. Through it, two generations give Phyllis their blessing.

After my mother's death, we adult children gathered to go over what remained in the family home to take what each of us wanted before the estate sale. I chose the well-worn hymnal that she used during her morning and evening meditation time. I was also curious to see what was in a particular drawer of her dresser that she always kept locked. I just knew that drawer had to contain treasure. I was right. I smiled as I surveyed its contents: homemade gifts from each of her four children before any of us were old enough to purchase presents. Completely without monetary value, they were all deeply cherished. I held in my hand a walnut shell, its halves lined with cotton overlaid in red satin to create a case for holding a ring. I gently put it back and asked my siblings if I could keep the key to that drawer. I have it with their blessing.

The key to my mother's heart sits on our fireplace mantel to this day, a continuous reminder of the true treasures in life. Like the pliers, that key takes up little space in our home but holds a central place in my heart. Nearby rest my grandfather's and my father's home communion sets, talismans of their vocations as Lutheran pastors and prophetic symbols of my own years in ministry, following in their footsteps. Like Phyllis, I have been upheld through the blessing of generations.

When Phyllis's mother died—the last to go of our parents—Phyllis chose to take the brass doorknobs from the family home that had been burdened under so much clutter and chaos amid the effects of alcoholism. Her brother took them off the doors for her. After careful cleaning, their beauty shines. Now installed in our own home, they are the perfect reframing of a house that was so closed in upon itself and so difficult to grow up in. They have been repurposed to symbolize the open door to love and hospitality. They remind us of her mother's faithful service of visitation to the elders in the nursing home across the street from the family home, an activity she kept up until she, too, moved into the nursing home shortly before her death. Each of our family homes has been demolished for the sake of new construction. There is no going back, only forward. It seems fitting for us. We have found home in the one we have made together.

Symbols help us make sense of the world around us and provide a shorthand for language. They take up little physical space but can hold volumes of meaning. Our home is rich in symbols that fill it with reminders of what is important in life. Can there be anything more valuable? I invite you to consider what you would keep, or pass on, that signifies the essence of your loved ones and the essence of who you are to your loved ones. In the smallest of things are meanings writ large.

19

Homes Occupied by Work and Electronics

Working from home, while often advantageous, also presents some challenges to family life. The 24/7 connectivity electronic devices offer provides flexibility of hours and convenience. However, they can also create some issues with respect to time, boundaries, and competition with family life. For families it can be confusing to know if a parent is considered "home" when working from home or "gone" with respect to taking interruptions to their work. If they feel ignored or devalued, young children and resentful spouses may be unable or unwilling to appreciate the difference between being *at* home and working *from* home. Pets, too, can act out after waiting in vain for a walk or playtime with their human guardians.

Another challenge when working from home is the issue of how physical space gets allocated to accommodate a home office. While a spare bedroom can be converted to workspace, many smaller homes don't offer that option. When other space is lacking, the dining room often gets conscripted for work purposes. This can have the domino effect of using the living room as the place for dining. When this occurs, the family no longer gathers around a table together enjoying good food and conversation, but instead sits around the TV. Very often, the quality of both conversation and food suffers, resulting in the loss of caring connections that can occur when people actually listen to one another and know what's going on in each other's lives.

What are the recourses? For some it's finding a coffee shop where they can combine work with refreshment; for others, cooperative use of rented office space works. At home it can easily sink into a "if you can't lick them, join them" situation where everyone may be in close proximity to one another, but each resorts to their own brand of concentrated distraction. The kids may be glued to video games while a parent is captive to work e-mails. The demarcation between when one is at work and when one is at home fades. So, too, does the attention we all need for our relationships to thrive.

My work in retirement has been providing childcare for our grandson while continuing to write. I manage the latter by getting up in the early morning hours to collect my thoughts before anyone else is awake. Then I snatch the hours of our grandson's naptime to be as productive as possible in my writing. I know I stand in a long line of women writers who spent lifetimes juggling domestic responsibilities with their passion to write. How people do this with more than one child, I cannot fathom, any more than I can fathom writing without the benefit of using a computer.

While there are occasional lapses, we all try not to bring our devices to a family dinner or accept calls or read text messages while eating together. Cooking is an activity in and of itself for Noelle and Evan, both of whom have worked in the food industry. The rest of us are the lucky beneficiaries of their culinary concoctions. Our little grandson has experienced a veritable cornucopia of tastes from the baby food his parents make for him. He already has a wider experience of ethnic foods in his short life than I did in the whole of my childhood. A musical little guy, Ciel loves to sing when enjoying food, a habit that warms my heart when remembering this similarity to my own childhood.

When our daughter was a child, she went back and forth between her moms' and her dads' households. Her dads, both excellent cooks, were formal diners and usually ate at the dining room table using lovely formal dinnerware. Her moms were not nearly as talented in the kitchen but enjoyed good simple food and more casual dining. Both households valued family meals together in their respective homes as well as dining together as a family of five. One day as our daughter was packing to spend the weekend with her dads, she remarked that she was looking forward to "dinner theater" with them that evening. When I asked where they were going, she replied, "Oh, we don't go anywhere, but on Fridays we get to have dinner in the living room. We eat on trays and watch a Disney movie together. It's so fun!" I suppressed my laughter and thought, *Clever dads! They have learned how to make watching TV a special treat.*

Later, when we moved back to Minnesota, we chose not to replace our television that had broken in transit. Instead, we had family outings designed to help our daughter get to know her new home. Later, as a working teen, she bought her own TV to play her favorite video game, but she has never been so captive to it that she couldn't enjoy a good book just as much. She recently commented that it still startles her to spend time in friends' homes where the TV is always on like white noise in the background, as family members all sit in the same room, everyone busily occupied with their personal devices. When this becomes the norm, we have lost the heart of our homes.

Homing together is not just a matter of sharing physical space but involves how we share time. It's interesting to see how frequently kids touch and interact with each other when they are playing outside or building a world with blocks or acting out their favorite action hero or creating a magic realm together. Virtual friendships cannot substitute for playdates with kids who are actually present, any more than electronics can substitute for special time with a parent who is untethered from their smartphone. For good or ill, our children are quick to pick up the behaviors we model. How are we using time together in our homes? With the availability electronics provide, when can we shut down and have time for solitude or time to enjoy spending with friends and loved ones? How can we protect the heart of our home while living in the digital age that has ushered in so many innovations along with so many distractions?

In our own home, we continue to struggle with these issues. Phyllis does most of her medical documentation at home in the evenings since spiritual care to people who are dying should not involve an open laptop at the bedside. The unfortunate consequence of this is that way too many of our evening hours are given over to her work, and Phyllis is deprived of time with the people she loves and counts on for renewal. So far, our best solution to this is to start the evening with supper (always on the patio during seasonable weather) when we catch up on each other's day. Later, we reserve an hour before bedtime for reading aloud, listening to music, or playing card games so she can relax and leave work out of her dreams.

Our household is certainly not free of electronics, nor do we seek to be. Food and electronics are also part of our get-togethers with our family of the heart. We gather for leisurely potluck dinners followed by a group viewing and discussion of a great TV series such as *Downton Abbey*, *Eyes on the Prize*, or *Angels in America*. This is one of the ways we stay abreast of each other's lives while also sharing lively and thoughtful entertainment.

It is important to regularly assess how electronics function in our lives as well as how working from home impacts family life. Are electronics drawing us together? What are we losing and what are we gaining by such connectivity? Do they expand our lives and our awareness of other cultures across the globe? Do they help us unite in our efforts to care for our planet and the magnificent creatures that are so vulnerable to human encroachment? Are they bringing education to children who might otherwise not have it? Do they promote healing and medical care in countries where doctors are scarce and medical facilities are few and far between? Are they keeping people whose work takes them abroad connected with their families? Who are we becoming as a society when electronics can be worn on our bodies and implanted within them?

Clearly, technology is here to stay and offers a wealth of educational, medical, and scientific advances as well as personal gratification. There is plenty of room for its contributions if we can use it mindfully while allowing space for nurturing our relationships. With so many things competing with family life, the bottom line is: Work in your home if you like, but don't let work become your home. Reach out to people across the globe via social media, but not at the expense of friends and family under the same roof. Enjoy virtual reality, but don't let it become your primary reality.

As a visitation pastor to homebound elders, my father spoke of a conversation he had with a woman near the end of her life. He had asked if she had any regrets. She replied, "Yes. As my friends got older and died, and my world narrowed, my biggest regret is that I wish I had laughed and cried more with real people than I have with fictional ones. It's easy to substitute TV families for real ones. But they're not the same."

There is no going back to a simpler time. But let's not forget the wonder of looking into each other's eyes, of holding a hand in difficult moments and experiencing our joys and sorrows in real time and space with each other. Author Maya Angelou, reflecting on life's meaning and value in an interview with Oprah Winfrey, once mused, "Do your eyes light up when your children walk into the room?" [15] How much Angelou's eyes lit up interacting with her own family was apparent from a statement made by her son, Guy Johnson, in his own interview with Oprah. He recalls how, over the years, many people have wondered what it was like to grow up in the shadow of a famous mother. To this he says, "I didn't grow up in her shadow. I grew up in her light." [16] Maya Angelou has shown us all why we are here: to offer one another shining eyes. This requires being awake and truly present to those moments when love slips into the room with us and seeks our company.

Creating Decor That Tells Your Story

In this day of interior designers, color consultants, and home design shows, there are a plethora of aids to creating home decor. However, creating your home's decor isn't only about hiring or watching professionals. While professionals can certainly be useful to consult, only the people who dwell in a home can ultimately determine what will make a house *their* home. Meaningful decor is what you create when you surround yourself with things that inspire, move, or uplift you and help you remember people and events precious to you.

The following examples and ideas are about self-expression and inspiration. They stem from our own process of creating home decor. We share them for your encouragement as you think about what you might create or choose for your home. This involves selecting things that reflect significant events, interests, or people you value. Sometimes, decor helps us solve a problem in our home spaces, reminding us that with problems comes opportunity. Other times, decor is about creatively repurposing things. Decor need not be expensive, but it does need to be personal. If our homes don't reflect us, whose are they?

For us, warm lighting, together with soft floor coverings that are comfortable for shoeless feet, are the starting point to creating our home's decor. From there, we have chosen to highlight those possessions that speak to who we are and what we value, individually and as a family. When selecting new artwork for our home, we invite people to participate in skill swapping with us as a way of mutually encouraging one another in creative expression. This has led to some wonderful additions to our home. To know the artisans that contribute to one's home is a rich experience that inspires one's own creativity and yields friendships with kindred spirits.

Three adventures in repurposing some of our home's furnishings in order to solve a problem have yielded good results. The first were the piano windows in our living room that gave us an unwanted view of our neighbors' roof after their tree was struck by lightning and removed. This prompted me to replace the clear glass with a design in stained glass that would allow light in but obscure the roof. For years we had collected stray prisms off old chandeliers and hung them from our curtain rods to catch the sun for an indoor rainbow effect. I decided to incorporate some of the prisms into my design for the piano windows. The result is a cascade of rainbows that dance across the walls throughout the day as the sun rises from the living room picture window, arcs across the dining room window, and sets in our kitchen window overlooking the garden spaces at day's end. Those rainbow prisms carry many associations for us, not least of which are the reminders of the abiding love and good humor of Noelle's fathers.

The second repurposing came about because the love seat and couch set we had owned for thirty years looked very out of place in our Craftsman-era home. Manufactured by a company that specialized in making indestructible dormitory furniture, their wood frames were a solid box design overlaid with foam cushions. We bought them because they were what we could afford at the time and because they provided excellent support for Phyllis, who has suffered back injury. They might as well have come with a lifetime warranty because the frames simply refused to show any significant signs of wear. They also fit perfectly in our relatively small living room space. That got me thinking, *What if my woodworker friend David could redesign our couch frames in the Craftsman style in exchange for a customized stained glass lamp for his home?* He enthusiastically agreed to this scheme, and the result surpassed both our expectations.

David now has a beautiful lamp for his living room, and we have a cleverly redesigned couch and love seat with reupholstered cushions befitting the style of our home. You would never guess their origins, nor could you tell that they weren't originally Craftsman by design. It was a delightful adventure in repurposing to great effect. In fact, the day of the Craftsman Bungalow Home Tour, one of the guests looked at our couches and exclaimed excitedly, "Is that furniture by *Stickley*?" We disabused him of that notion by showing him the "before and after" photos of the conversion that led to the low-budget version of "Stickley by David."

The third adventure in successful repurposing came from missing having a fireplace in our home. We decided to order an electric fireplace with a handsome oak mantel that perfectly matched our home's oak woodwork. Unfortunately, the firebox had a cheesy faux slate surround that cheapened the look of the otherwise beautiful mantel. Luckily, I was able to find stained glass that looked very similar to the traditional fireplace tiles of the Craftsman era. I replaced the faux slate with stained glass tiles and framed them in brass. Then I overlaid the tiles with brass stampings depicting nature motifs in keeping with the period. The effect is vintage charm.

In all three cases, problem-solving became an opportunity for successful customizing. We received many compliments on the couches, the mantel, and the piano windows during the tour with several requests to take photographs, which we readily granted. We finished off our open plan living room/dining room space courtesy of a church garage sale that yielded six oak dining room chairs built in the 1920s that perfectly complement our oak table. Now that they are complete, our furnishings look as at home in our setting as we feel.

The works of art in our home have found their rightful places too. Over the hearth in our living room hangs a painting depicting the "Flight into Egypt" by American artist John August Swanson. This story from Christian Scripture recounts the narrow escape of the infant Jesus from the threat of assassination by King Herod, a ruler determined to rid himself of what he believes is a future competitor to his throne. As the little family of Joseph, Mary, and Jesus (held protectively in his mother's arms) leaves Bethlehem in the dead of night, one can see soldiers in distant pursuit. The family is forced to flee—like so many refugees of today—exiled from their home country, stumbling along a narrow path, yet guided by the light of angels they cannot see. As viewers, we can see the assistance offered to them and are reminded that in times of crisis, we, too, have unseen hands lighting our way when our world is dark and hope is lost. We are also reminded to embody those hands for those who are in need of safety and shelter.

A second painting hanging over our oak buffet was purchased from a gallery of donated works, the proceeds of which were being given to build a new hospice in San Francisco for people with AIDS. It was the same hospice Phyllis later served as a volunteer chaplain providing spiritual care and comfort to its residents. The artist was a man who died of AIDS shortly before the gallery showing. His painting captures a beautiful view of the city from one of the steep hills along Dolores Street. The fog rolls slowly in over the late afternoon sun still shining off the city skyline. This painting holds memories—exquisitely joyful and ineffably sad—of our years living in San Francisco.

A third painting, rendered by my artist sister-in-law, Nanci Yermakoff, depicts our family cabin on a lake in northern Minnesota, whose rustic hospitality has now blessed four generations. From inside the cozy cabin, the viewer looks out at a winter landscape in the woods. You can almost "hear" the stillness of snowfall. Every time we look at it, we are transported from the clamor of city life to the magic of that special place of connection to the natural world. Just gazing at that scene provides its own brief experience of renewal.

On our living room wall hangs a reverie harp, the instrument Phyllis uses in her work as a hospice chaplain. With it, she brings comfort to those patients and families who are facing significant life changes as well as their own mortality. The harp speaks to the many who have peacefully made their passage from this world, accompanied by its music and the whispered expressions of love and blessing from family members. The harp sings to us even when silent. It affirms our belief that love attends us wherever we go. At night, Noelle's fathers have wrapped all of us in their love through the gift of beautiful quilts designed and made by Jay with Ched's assistance.

Noelle and Evan express their creativity through the aromatic and delicious foods they serve. Our grandson, Ciel, enlivens our home by being intensely interested and curious about everything: tasting, touching, taking apart, and playing with whatever he encounters. For him, everything is a toy or a new experience. One of his favorite pastimes is to locate all the rainbows cast on the walls by our piano window prisms so that he can gently pat those within his reach. He inspires us to interact more with each other and to notice our environment.

These descriptions of decor are to encourage you to be bold in making decor your own through whatever avenue of creativity you choose. We all have creativity within us of one sort or another. Whether it is visual arts or culinary creations, designs in fabric or woodworking, gardening or music making, we can encourage, inspire, and uplift one another. Decor is our story expressing itself through our dwellings and the people in our lives. It is also our link with those loved ones who have traveled this earthly path before us and whose love shines on us when we have trouble finding our way in the dark.

PART FOUR

FORMING AND SUPPORTING FAMILIES

"Family is two or more persons who share resources, share responsibility for decisions, share values and goals, and have commitments to one another over time. The family is the climate that one 'comes home to,' and it is this network of sharing and commitments that most accurately describes the family unit, regardless of blood, legalities, adoption, or marriage." [17]

"Call it a clan, call it a network, call it a tribe, call it a family: whatever you call it . . . you need one."

~ Jane Temple Howard, *Families* [18]

21

Choosing Families of the Heart

A large part of "homing" in any locale is the people who travel with us and the people we seek out in friendship. Ideally, our first family gives us our first experience of nurture. This equips us to grow up strong and secure in their love, enabling us to weather the seas of life with the ability to add more avenues for friendship and love however far we travel. Most families of origin do the best they can by us. But there are many whose best efforts fell short of what their children needed to fully thrive. Of course there are outside wreckers of family security too: economic injustice, displacement in time of war, vulnerability to diseases of addiction or mental illness, as well as racism, heterosexism, and all the other "isms" that jeopardize health and well-being.

For some people, neglect, abuse, or abandonment was the primary experience within their families of origin. Less drastically, but still harmful, are parental expectations that are misaligned with their child's sense of self or core identity. This is especially true for young people who are struggling to come to terms with their sexual orientation or gender identity. This can undermine safety and well-being into adulthood.

Sometimes adults slip into what was familiar to them in childhood, repeating the mistakes of their parents in their own parenting. It's easy to bring unwanted baggage with us. This is why it's important for adults to seek the help of trained professionals who can offer tools for strengthening and respecting boundaries—our own and those of our children. Healthy choices in family life can get an assist from early childhood education classes, or the extended hand of friendship from another parent who can mentor a different approach, or the honesty of a Twelve Step group, or the sanctuary of those who share our struggle for authentic identity. Whatever the avenue for health and healing, we must choose with care and with intentionality. Everyone deserves a loving family.

Families of the heart can build on positive experiences from one's first family as well as help us reframe and overcome negative experiences. They can even help heal the deep wounds of outright rejection from our families of origin. So how do we find or form our own family of the heart? While there is no template for this, we can start where we are most connected to others. It may be coworkers whom we see regularly, or it may be neighbors or members of our faith community. Sometimes it's people who come together over a common social cause or volunteer service work. Other times it happens in shared recreational pursuits such as a garden club or a sports group.

Occasionally, families of the heart are right in front of you but have never been identified as such. A good start is to think about the people currently involved in your life. What do they bring to you? Do they bring out the best in you? Do they dare to lovingly confront you when you begin to veer off course from how you want to live or when you are drawn to a relationship that may be harmful to you? Are they there for you when you're sick or going through a hard time and need some tender loving care? Sometimes, ties that have already been formed with someone can be further strengthened by simply naming who you already are to each other.

Years ago, my former college roommate asked me to be a godparent to one of her sons. We didn't live close to one another and hadn't seen one another often, but being asked to fill that role made me realize how important Sally was to me and I to her. I wish I could say I was a good godparent with a close relationship with my godchild, neither of which I can claim through no fault of his. But it did deepen a relationship with his mother that has been precious to me over the years. It has been continuously nourished by that initial honor and her faithfulness in calling me every year on my birthday. I truly consider Sally family of the heart despite our geographical distance. Our annual conversations have become a yearly mini "life review" that I look forward to and count on each December.

One year, I was deeply saddened to receive a call from Sally informing me of the death of her older son and honored that she wanted me to say a few words at his memorial. On first meeting, we can't know who we will become to one another, but we must be ready to be chosen and bold in choosing. Sally is my role model for constancy in friendship and courage in the face of unspeakable sorrow. She is a gift to those she loves. And as a medical professional who tirelessly advocates on behalf of her patients, she is a gift to those she serves. Carrying the daily burden of grief, she is unstinting in her commitment to making a difference in the world. She is one of my oldest friends and will always have a place in my heart.

Sometimes we find ourselves in a time of life when it is hard to identify who could be family of the heart to us. However we go about choosing, we don't need to start with groups of people who all know each other well. Nor does our family of the heart group need to be lifelong. It may be for an important season of life. We can begin forming a group by starting with one person we know and trust. That person can invite another person they know and trust. It only takes three people to form a group of six. The group can remain at that size or grow at will over time.

A commitment to meet once a month over six months gives the group a chance to coalesce and determine how viable it is to continue meeting beyond the sixth month. If a couple of participants choose to drop out, the others can decide if they want to add new members or continue meeting as is.

A family group may also be formed over a common experience, such as cooking together and enjoying a shared meal monthly. Or it can form around a need, such as neighbors who rally around someone in their community who is going through a debilitating illness and needs assistance with meals, childcare, or property maintenance. A group formed around parenting may include children.

Recently, I was a guest at a monthly gathering of parents who spend the first hour of their time playing together with the children and their second hour meeting privately to share the joys and problems of parenting. As the parents meet, their children continue to play while being watched by a couple of nannies funded cooperatively by all the parents. While they hadn't consciously designated themselves a family of choice, it was evident that the parents had seen one another through difficult times with their children and had formed supportive family bonds together.

Before we became parents, Phyllis and I initiated an informal support group for same-gender couples that turned into a three-year experience of becoming family of the heart together, sharing meals and outings and vacation retreats. That group helped us realize what can happen when people intentionally name what they have become to one another and what that means together. Our current family of the heart in Minnesota has met regularly for twelve years now, in the process weathering some transitions of its group members over the years. Serendipity combines with intentionality when forming and maintaining families of the heart. The key is to be ready, flexible, and mindful of where the opportunities lie for such possibilities. If we are open to them, life gives us plenty of opportunities to risk reaching out to cultivate deeper connections with others.

In the early stages of group formation, it's helpful to share what your hopes and expectations are for how you may wish the group to function in your lives. Careful listening is essential for understanding, so some friendly ways of containing the extroverts and encouraging the introverts should be considered. (I speak as an extrovert who feels well loved by our group but has needed to take care to respect space and listening time for my much-cherished but more introverted friends.) It is also good to determine whether your group is closed or open and the time frames for either one of those options. Groups need time to gel, but closed groups can lose oxygen if not renewed by "new blood." Transitions will occur one way or another, whether through geographical mobility or relationship dissolutions or just a sense of no longer needing or desiring to continue in a group. It is important to be open to and flexible with life changes without judgment. Life changes can be painful, but they are also inevitable. We cannot require our loved ones to forego change any more than we can require it of ourselves.

It is this kind of intentionality that we need to bring to our efforts when choosing who shall constitute our families of the heart. As we think about the influences in our lives from those we have invited into our hearts, we need to ask ourselves, "Is this a life-giving relationship of love and respect that calls out and affirms the best of me?" "Do I like who I am with these people?" "Am I accepted without judgment and valued for my integrity when I show my vulnerabilities and speak with authenticity?" "Do my friends care about working for a kinder and more just world?" If the answer is a resounding "Yes!" we have chosen wisely. Today, our own families of the heart are scattered across a wide geography, expanding our hearts with every move and every home.

22

Becoming Family

Introduction

This is an interview with the author's family of the heart. The members of this family are made up of two single individuals, Robbyn and Phoebe, and two couples, Lynn and Sherry, and Phyllis and Ruth. The group has been meeting approximately every two months for fifteen years. It has varied in size over time. Transitions occasioned by changes in relationship or geographical moves have occurred periodically over the years. In this conversation, we reflect on how we became family of the heart and what "homing" means to us. We also acknowledge a recent transition that was difficult for us. The author is both interviewer and participant.

RUTH: One of the things I so appreciate about our family of the heart is how much it expands my notions of family. As a society, I think we are beginning to think more generously about who is family. When we are open to expanding families beyond those of marital partnerships or first families, we have rich possibilities. Let's talk a bit about what it has meant to be family of the heart to one another. Thinking back, how did we get started?

LYNN: You two were the magnet that drew us together in the beginning and started what we decided to call ourselves: family of the heart. The more time we had together, the more important we became to each other. We also had some spiritual history, but it was how much we enjoyed each other and our shared values that became the glue that held us together. We got closer as we committed to celebrating some major holidays too. I think time and intention furthered our relationships quite naturally. While it's true we chose one another in the beginning, our choice deepened as we connected more and more from the heart. In the process, we *became* family of the heart.

SHERRY: Having people who know what's going on in your life, whether it's your health issues, your job, or your kids, makes such a difference. One of the things I also value about this group is that we are close, but our hospitality is open. We have been willing to fold new people into our group and invest time and care in each other. But nothing stays the same. Our lives go through different seasons of change, as well as geographical change when people move or couples break up. Sometimes a season is simply fulfilled and moving on is just natural.

ROBBYN: Throughout my childhood and adolescence, we moved a lot, so what stayed constant was my family. That kept us pretty dependent on each other. The fact that my father was a pastor made it harder because no kids wanted to play at the preacher's house. Growing up in my family as part of majority culture also contributed to my loneliness because I believed I was the only family member who didn't really belong in that culture. Years later I learned this wasn't true when my younger sister came out as lesbian. But this early awareness of my "difference" made me determined to claim my freedom to choose the family I needed as an adult.

PHYLLIS: For a kid, that was a pretty advanced level of self-awareness, Robbyn!

RUTH: And here we all are! I'm not sure if you chose us or we chose you, but I'm sure glad it happened and am so grateful for this family. When I think about the years I spent trying to pass as straight, it pains me. What saved me was being introduced to the early sanctuary movement for LGBT people in those Lutheran churches that first "came out" to gays and lesbians as "reconciling congregations." To have a place to worship and socialize under the protection of confidentiality helped me let down my guard and begin trusting. It gave me a chance to practice authenticity. It was still a closet, but it was a lot bigger than my personal closet.

LYNN: Yes, that's part of our early, shared history together that eventually led to our bond today. We didn't know each other well back then, but we felt safe together, and that helped form our friendship. Ultimately, authenticity always leads to greater freedom and intimacy.

RUTH: So, how do you think family of the heart is different from just having good friends?

SHERRY: It's the glue and the history you build over time. You count on regular time together. And you build events and rituals together, whether it's watching a good TV series or reading a good book or going to a play together. Whatever you are doing creates history together. You come to understand and rely on and accept one another.

LYNN: It's the grace and nonjudgment of family of the heart that I love. We can dive deep together, or just eat and laugh together. There's a freedom with family of the heart that you don't always have with other friends.

PHYLLIS: When we say, "You are family of the heart to me," we are automatically saying, "You are important to me." Something happens when you are intentional about letting someone know, "This is who you are to me." And it's not about holding anyone prisoner. It's just not withholding what someone means to you. What you are really saying is, "This being together is worth investing in."

PHOEBE: Being single all my life, I have valued being part of all of you. When you're single, you work hard to fit into other people's lives. Having family of the heart is a relief because it's having a place of belonging with people you respect and have come to know over meals and holidays and rituals and shared friendship. You don't have to work at it so much. After a while, the group has its own energy together.

PHYLLIS: While we are based in friendship, we move to another level in being family. When you are family, you are in it together. There is some core stability in seeing one another as family. Family just *is*.

RUTH: How does creating intentional family help heal the wounds of first family?

SHERRY: It gives you another chance, a different way, and a different choice. It means acceptance without conditions.

ROBBYN: Having this family "norms" my life experience in a way my first family couldn't for a long time. Even though my parents have supported me for many years now, it was still hard to talk to them about my breakup with Ann. After investing a lot in helping parents understand and accept same-gender partnerships, you worry about disappointing them if you break up. But even within *this* group, I have to say it was hard to talk about breaking up because Ann and I had been in this family of the heart together.

RUTH: That's certainly understandable. It got complicated for us, too, because things were pretty up and down between the two of you for quite a while. We couldn't tell if we were standing by to support you in staying together or in uncoupling.

ROBBYN: I didn't know at first either.

LYNN: In different ways, everyone got thrown into a situation where the future was uncharted territory, and that's always an uncomfortable place to be.

SHERRY: Lynn and I were sad for both of you. And we struggled with how to be with each of you singly. It didn't help that we were preparing for our wedding at that time, which made it even harder. We didn't know if we should invite both you and Ann to our wedding or just one of you, and we knew it would be hard either way.

PHYLLIS: We wanted to try to hold space for each of you separately, outside the family of the heart group. We knew you both needed safety to talk confidentially with us. I can see now how it became a balancing act that got in the way of being fully present to you.

ROBBYN: I can understand that. But one thing that could have happened is for this family of the heart to have offered a ritual acknowledging our breakup after Ann moved away. That would have been helpful.

RUTH: That's a very good point. And we didn't. I wish we had.

ROBBYN: I remember being part of a ritual of "unbinding" that a woman in my human sexuality class had for herself when she separated from her husband. While it was painful, it really helped her. But I didn't quite know how to ask for that.

PHOEBE: I'm wondering, would it be helpful to you if we had such a ritual now, Robbyn, just for you? Or are we too late?

ROBBYN: I think it would still be helpful.

PHYLLIS: Let's plan a ritual at our next gathering then. (There is general consensus for this.) Thank you for helping us learn how we can do a better job of offering support, Robbyn.

RUTH: Can we talk for a few moments about what spirituality and "homing" mean to us?

SHERRY: Well, one of the things spirituality has meant to me is that we can talk when we feel like it and ask for prayer when we need it. It's good to be able to count on that regardless of what form it takes.

PHYLLIS: Yes, I like that we try to hold space for each other's troubles and for healing.

RUTH: How do you think sharing family of the heart affects "homing"?

PHOEBE: Family of the heart is a place of belonging just as home is a place of refuge.

PHYLLIS: You all know I grew up in a family home that was a wreck instead of a refuge. That's part of what makes it so good to be in each other's homes and celebrate in them. It resets my old experience of home. I like to see the different ways each of us is homing.

PHOEBE: I have never considered space my own. First I shared my home with roommates, and for the past many years, with my sister. I am realizing that I have used my home mainly just to rest and regroup in order to keep up with the demands of life. Now that I'm retired, I want to begin reclaiming the gift of home by opening it up to others more. It feels like I have often been tied up with my family's activities. But I do want to help them when they need me. And, of course, there are times when I need them.

RUTH: I think we all want to be there for friends and family when they need us. But it's important to count *yourself* among the people you love. Phoebe, my hope for you is that you will give yourself permission to live into this gift of time. I have learned that it takes a while to figure out your new life in retirement and the opportunities that come with it.

ROBBYN: These days I'm doing a lot of thinking about how to identify who is a peer so I can pick friendships on the basis of being peers and have fewer relationships based primarily on trying to help others. It's an issue of balance, I think, especially because my work involves so much therapeutic support to clients.

PHYLLIS: It's also easy for those of us who are partnered to think of those of you who are single as more readily available. But both of you have had very demanding jobs in the medical profession that didn't permit much time for yourselves. It makes the challenge of finding balance even more important. As we talk of homing, I think of you, too, Sherry, and how your health challenges have increasingly caused you to become more homebound. How do you not feel trapped in your own home but grounded in it?

SHERRY: Well, having the dogs helps me. They're good company.

PHYLLIS: I know the dogs love to snuggle with you when you need to rest and have coaxed you outside when you needed to get out. All of us want to visit, but it's harder to know when to call on you without disturbing your rest.

SHERRY: Yes, and when you do visit, I don't want to fall asleep on you like I did with Ruth the other day.

PHYLLIS: Oh, we've all done that! (The group laughs.)

LYNN: We appreciate all of you coming to us when Sherry doesn't have the energy to come to you. We try to surround ourselves with people we love who share our values. We also take pride in our home space. I like that I can sit anywhere in this space and see something we love—whether an interior designer would like it, I don't know. But if you look at our things, I think you get a good sense of who we are and what's important to us.

SHERRY: As the range of my outside environment has gotten smaller, we've tried to maintain the inside positively. When Phyllis was talking about the house she grew up in, I thought about mine and how I, too, never invited anyone home because—oh, my God, they would know our family secrets! So now Lynn and I try to practice hospitality in our home as much as we can to experience the joy of being openhearted with our home.

RUTH: Your home is a big part of the hospitality we receive. Meeting in each other's homes has made me appreciate the creativity in this group. You know I'm a big fan of "show and tell." While we need to get together to talk about what concerns us, I love that we also celebrate creativity because it's so essential to joy. I'm always glad to see your creations in jewelry and fabric, Robbyn, and your photography, Lynn. I love sharing one of your wonderful barbecues, Sherry, and nestling into your outdoor reading nook under the pines, Phoebe. At Christmas I look forward to having you all over when Phyllis shares her latest carol with us. We are connected by what we share, by the people we love and the light we bring into the world. When I look at the stained glass in our home, it makes me happy to know each of your homes has a lamp made by me—because you all bring light into my life and into the world. Thank you for this time together.

Animal Companions as Family

When we are very small, it's likely that our first soft "cuddly" is not a doll but an animal tucked under the covers with us when it's time to go to sleep. Toy animals as companions go as far back as our pre-language selves.

My first animal companion was a red elephant stuffed with sawdust, given to me by my aunt when I was four years old. I named him Tippy. He had a characteristic that I esteemed highly, which was that when I turned a brass key sticking out of his back, he "sang" Brahms's "Lullaby" for me. I didn't think of him as a toy with a music box inside him but as an animal friend who faithfully sang to me every night. I don't think there was ever an evening I didn't turn that key and fall asleep to the comfort of his melody. Like the bunny in the children's book *The Velveteen Rabbit*, Tippy became "real" by having all his soft "skin" rubbed threadbare from loving hugs. Whenever I slept away from the comforts of home, Tippy brought a bit of home with him each night he sang for me. He is still part of my childhood experience of family, though his elephant self wore out from all my childhood loving. Over the years, he lost much of his sawdust stuffing as well as his shoe-button eyes, but still I cherished him in his blind state.

In adulthood, I finally gave up his disintegrated body but retained his musical soul that is miraculously still singing over sixty-five years later. His music box has been embedded within a beautiful handmade oak mantel clock. We have dubbed it our "time and eternity" clock, as it holds within its chamber Tippy's song and several small items that have precious sentimental and spiritual value to us. While we can't tuck Tippy in bed with our grandson, Ciel has his own companion in the form of a sea turtle whose shell glows with a soft underwater light effect. With the help of an embedded microchip, the turtle provides the soothing sounds of ocean waves from the womb of Mother Earth, gently lulling him asleep.

When I was six, we got our first family dog, an Irish setter named Flame. I have fond memories of taking afternoon naps with Flame, curled up against her flank with my ear pressed close to the beat of her heart. A year later, after she had given birth to eleven puppies, I remember crawling into her kennel with the puppies, unsuccessfully trying to scoop them all up so I could hold them together. "I wish I had a thousand arms!" my father later recalled me exclaiming. That was the beginning of a lifelong love affair with dogs, shared with my brother, John, who only half-facetiously maintains that if there is life on the other side, he wants to meet all his beloved dogs in one fine pack first. The humans can wait their turn to greet him.

While working as a hospice chaplain, I had the pleasure of doing some co-visits with our pet therapist to those patients who had requested pet therapy. At her signal, Frankie carefully crawled into bed with them and, guided by her, would gently snuggle against whatever part of their body could sustain light pressure without causing pain. Even patients close to death would sometimes open their eyes at the gentle touch of his soft muzzle. A smile would play across their face, and their labored breathing would slow into a relaxed rhythm that could carry them across the threshold with a last peaceful exhale.

Years ago, we had a family dog that displayed similar empathic characteristics. We had started a book group that was meeting monthly in our home. At our second meeting, one of the members tearfully confided to the group that his partner had just left him. Jenna, who was not allowed up on our living room furniture, immediately got up from her place by my chair and walked over to this man she did not know, placed her head on his knee, and simply gazed into his eyes soulfully. From that meeting on, she voluntarily lay by him, gently resting her head on his foot.

Jenna practiced this same concern when our daughter had occasional nightmares as a child and would cry out in her sleep. Since her room was down the hall from us, we sometimes didn't hear her right away. But Jenna would come into our bedroom and nudge Phyllis to wake up and go check on our girl.

Anyone who has watched a service dog at work, or who has experienced the comfort of a pet growing up when adults may not have consistently been there for them, knows the power animals have to keep us connected to a lifeline of unconditional love. Sometimes, the heart of our home is the faithful love and devotion given to us by our pets, some of which are capable of putting to shame our own best efforts at unconditional love. To this day, I cannot resist the financial appeals from organizations concerned with the possible extinction of elephants in our lifetime, thanks to the comfort given a small child by a toy musical elephant. As to dogs, I wouldn't be without one!

Protecting Intimacy in Partnerships

A house doesn't fully become a home until it has been shared with those we love. While it is important to talk about family in a way that reaches beyond the traditional views of marriage, it is also important to affirm the unique challenges and rewards that come with long-term partnerships and marital relationships. From our work in support of couples and from our own experience as a couple that has been together for thirty-six years, we have developed a list of tips in support of healthy partnerships. We are indebted to those that have contributed to this list over the years.

These tips are not in lieu of receiving help from a good counselor. Sometimes outside eyes and new tools are needed to assess what direction to take with seemingly insoluble problems. We know this from our own experience as a couple who utilized counseling to get through the rough spots of parenthood and also to strengthen our family bond with our daughter's dads. If you show up with a willingness to grow and a resolve to rediscover and affirm the good in one another, counseling can be an effective tool for renewing and deepening a relationship. However, we do not advocate staying in a relationship that threatens either party's emotional or physical well-being. Nor do we advocate staying in a therapeutic relationship that is not client centered and respectful of each one's personhood.

These insights are offered with good wishes for their success, and the caveat to remember that everyone is a work in progress until the day they die.

Eleven Tips for Healthy Partnerships

1. Let your home reveal who you are together and what is important to you.

Decide how you want your home to function and what you want others to experience in it. Create space for hospitality, play, rest, romance, and creative renewal. Surround yourselves with symbols of what is important to both of you. Let your home reflect your values, your interests, and your relationships. If you work from home, don't let work *become* your home.

2. Let money serve your values and partner your dreams.

Consider enlisting the help of a life coach or financial planner who can help you determine how to use your finances to reflect your values, maximize your goals, plan for the future, and leave a legacy of love. Invest your time, energy, good will, and money in ways that reflect what matters to you. Make a contribution with your partnership. Identify a cause you both care about and volunteer some time to it. The index for happiness isn't how much money we make but how we spend our time. Money we earn. Time is a gift.

3. Listen generously—without making judgments or unilaterally imposing solutions.

Allow feelings to be messengers that have something important to convey. Pay attention to the needs that underlie feelings. Be aware of your body language and what it is conveying. Stay focused on one issue at a time. Reflect back what you are hearing to check if you are hearing accurately and fully. When you listen from the heart, people will speak from the heart.

4. Express your feelings directly.

State your feelings and own them ("*I* feel hurt when . . .") without linking them to blame or making your partner responsible for how you feel ("*You* make me feel angry when . . ."). Identify your desired outcome. It's not about being right. It's about being real and being willing to be vulnerable in order to further understanding. Remember, it's when we are convinced we are right that we are apt to be the most hurtful because that's when we feel most righteous.

5. Fight fair, fight seldom, and don't go to bed angry.

Select your battles carefully and sparingly. Be aware of the tone and volume of your voice. Tone speaks far louder than words. Establish ground rules for conflict when you're *not* fighting. Identify triggers that jeopardize feeling safe and devise a plan to preserve safety. Stick to one or two issues at a time. It's too demoralizing to tackle a host of issues together. Establish appropriate time-outs and reentry points. Seek win-win outcomes rather than entrenching right/wrong positions.

6. Convey appreciation three times as much as you express criticism.

Notice small kindnesses but let go of small annoyances. Never offer appreciation followed by "but." Appreciation must stand by itself or it will not be heard. Offer non-blaming, constructive feedback. Identify what obstacle stands in the way of a better result that both of you can be happier with by overcoming.

7. Keep the flair in your affair; prioritize time together and plan surprises.

Establish a regular "date night." Take turns planning a day trip with a surprise destination or activity for you and your partner to enjoy. Turn off electronic devices when dining or on a date. The end of the day when you are tired is not the time for raising hot-button issues, but if one crops up, set a time to talk that will work for both of you. Remove the TV and any reminders of work or previous relationships from your bedroom. Reserve the bedroom for rest, romance, and renewal.

Relationships, past and present, are resources for love and learning. Consider honoring some of them by giving them space elsewhere in the home. Hallways are transitional passageways that make good memorabilia photo walls. If children want to have certain photos in their personal spaces, respect their wishes. Photo albums or digital picture frames can preserve important memories in limited space.

8. Choose friends and family wisely.

Recognizing that no one relationship "completes" us, pick friendships with people who support you as a couple/family and who affirm you as individuals. In addition to enjoying the support of your first family, choose people (ideally in geographical proximity) whom you identify as your family of the heart. Let them know what they mean to you so you can be intentional in your support of one another.

9. Accept one another, forgive one another, and bless one another.

Grace and gift are the context of our intimate relationships. Since we don't earn love or gain worth from outward approval, we are free to dig deeper for resources of connection and growth. Core acceptance, laced with generous amounts of kindness, is essential for building trust. We all make mistakes and hurt each other, so it's important to leave the path open to giving and receiving forgiveness. It is the only way to receive important lessons, let go of deep hurts, and make new beginnings. We must consciously look for the good in each other and bless it.

10. Enjoy the journey and trust the outcome.

Invest in the quality of your commitment and your process together, and you will discover that longevity and destination will take care of themselves. Live the truth of your lives with thoughtful examination as well as forgiveness. Seek help if something holds you captive to the past. New chapters cannot fix old ones, but they can offer comfort and perspective as well as understanding. In doing so, they help refocus energy on the present, which is where we are meant to live. In the words of Francis Bacon, "Begin doing what you want to do now. . . . We have only this moment, sparkling like a star in our hand—and melting like a snowflake." [19] Amid the changes and chances of life, authenticity, faithfulness, forgiveness, and openheartedness form the framework for growth. Within that framework, we can also immediately begin being what we hope to become.

11. Choose a theme for your life together as inspiration for the road.

Revisit it when you celebrate your anniversary and see if it still speaks to you. Make adaptations if you wish or adopt a new one as desired. Think of it as a mini life review, with the focus on your life together. In life's final analysis, "I did it my way" is overrated. "With help, we find our way together" is what counts. We have chosen our theme without changes, but at times it has been a big gulp of life to swallow. Thirty-four years later, we still find it worthwhile to keep trying to live into it: *For all that has been—Thanks. To all that shall be—Yes!* [20]

25

Crossing Life Thresholds

Our grandson is beginning to put names and nouns to people and things. As soon as he wakes up in the morning, Ciel orients to the day and his surroundings by pointing to every object he can see, asking to know its name. Then he wants to be held up to the buffet where there is a small collection of brass bells on display. He likes that they each have a handle with an animal on it and is fascinated with the different tones each bell makes. So if anyone misses their morning alarm, Ciel will usher us into the day with bells.

When coming in from outside, Ciel points to the brass knocker on our front door and wants to be lifted up to use it. He raises its heavy arm and bangs it down with a satisfying *thwack,* announcing his arrival before he walks in. A milestone was reached this week when he came in from the winter cold and walked across the threshold. Holding my partner's hand, he looked up and exclaimed cheerfully, "Home!" It warmed our hearts to have confirmation that he recognizes where and with whom he belongs, and that in crossing our threshold he knows he has come home.

I have been thinking a lot lately about thresholds. Now seventy years old, when I cross a threshold to get something from another room, half the time I have forgotten what I came for once I get there. I have to turn around and go back in order to remember it before I can complete moving forward. Perhaps there's a lesson in this beyond encroaching senility. When considering life as our story, it may be appropriate to forget some of the chapters we leave behind in order to turn our faces toward what comes next. But the threshold experience requires us to reconnect with the past in order to retrieve what is valuable before moving into the future. That may be particularly true for painful things in our past. Forgetting isn't an on-off switch. It's a conscious letting go, after carefully considering what to keep and what to entrust to a greater Wisdom.

One of the things I have been trying to reconnect with more realistically is my history as a poliomyelitis survivor from early childhood. "Aging in place" has become more of an issue for me than I have wanted to admit. Two recent knee replacement surgeries have reminded me to prepare proactively for the eventuality of more serious physical limitations. Although I walk with an obvious limp, I generally have chosen not to volunteer the information that I had polio unless asked. I have not wanted to make much of it because remembering the worst parts of the experience and the surgeries and therapies that were necessary for my recovery puts me in touch with my vulnerability. I also dislike identifying as "handicapped" because of its pejorative association with weakness and being regarded as "less than" fully able-bodied people.

My experience of polio necessitated three hospitalizations: the first at age four, the second at seven accompanied by surgery, and the third at eleven for another surgery. Each hospitalization included various kinds of physical therapy. Before any treatments could begin during the first hospitalization, I was required to spend a week in isolation at the onset of the illness to reduce the risk of contagion to others. No one was allowed in my room save nurses, doctors, and aides. The separation from anyone I knew was underscored by the fact that those I didn't know were all white gowned, gloved, and masked and never stayed more than a few minutes. About midweek, another masked person came into the isolation unit and told me my parents were there to visit me but needed to visit while standing outdoors so they wouldn't "catch your flu."

She took me out of my crib and lifted me up to the window. There, four stories below, stood the small figures of my mother and father, my dad waving his hat and my mother vigorously waving her white handkerchief up at me. I took one look and burst into tears. I was admonished not to cry so I wouldn't upset my parents who had driven from Decorah, Iowa, to Rochester, Minnesota, to catch a glimpse of me. I was incapable of stopping my tears and felt terrible that I couldn't. It seemed like a serious failure on my part. The negative takeaway for me was to forever after curb any impulse to give in to tears no matter what the situation called for. "Don't cry, be strong" was further reinforced by the frenetic atmosphere of a medical system overwhelmed by the epidemic. Everyone feared contagion, and no one had time for emotional support. There were just too many of us. On the last day of isolation, a crib was brought into the isolation room with a small baby in it, another victim of polio. I was sad to find out babies got polio too. As I was transferred from the isolation area to the children's ward, I was further dismayed to see tiny "iron lungs"—the early version of ventilators—lining the hallways, waiting for their infant occupants.

On our children's ward, there was another child a little younger than I who cried every night for her mother, who also had polio. Sometimes she would call out my name as well, I think because we were the youngest children in the ward at the time. Over and over, I would hear "Rufie, Rufie, help!" I wanted her to stop, but she didn't. After a while, I stopped hearing her. I had grown numb. When my father visited, I told him about her and confessed my silence. He gently reminded me that her family couldn't visit. From then on, he divided his time between me and the other children who were not receiving many visits from family. Learning their names, he would go around the ward, pausing at bedsides to offer gentle words of encouragement and a listening ear. I remember having divided feelings of resentment about sharing him and pride that he was my father.

One day, I received an unexpected visit from my alcoholic uncle who showed up with an armload of toys that he dumped into the crib I briefly shared with another child. His breath smelled of booze as he leaned over and shouted, "How are ya, Ruthie? These are for you!" And with that he was gone, never to return again, but having dropped a bit of heaven on us in passing.

The most powerful visceral memory of hospitalization was that of pain. By age eleven, I needed extensive reconstructive surgery on my leg and foot that involved some bone fusion and tendon transfers to replace main tendons that could no longer do their job. The pain of that work was greater than anything I had ever experienced before or since. It was the kind of pain that makes it impossible to concentrate on anything else, that makes you so desperate for relief that nothing and no one in the world matters anymore.

Surviving polio has given me a keen respect for the toll physical pain takes on the human spirit as well as the body. My experiences of polio engendered a kind of stoicism on my part that has proved to be both a strength and a liability. At the time, I really didn't have a choice. I did not learn until years after contracting polio that one of our most beloved presidents—Franklin Delano Roosevelt—was a polio survivor who served this country and its war-torn world with distinction for an unprecedented twelve years. He, like I, also did not wish his life story to become a polio story and hid as much of it as he could so as not to jeopardize his political career.

As I look back on this now, I realize how many good people put themselves and their families in harm's way in order to treat us. I remember one of the nurses telling us that a doctor who made rounds on our ward had a wife and daughter who were both hospitalized with polio. There were nuns who also made daily visits to provide spiritual comfort. They had a gentle way of smoothing our pillows and offering a kind word with a quick prayer before moving on to the scores of other bedridden patients. Those moments of motherly comfort felt like a touch of home to me. I will always carry a debt of gratitude for those nuns. They were a manifestation of love.

I was proud of my recovery from polio and to have moved through surgeries, to wheelchair, to brace, to crutches, and finally to walking confidently without aids. But pride is dangerous when used comparatively. I have always fully understood that those who did not experience my level of recovery had no responsibility for that. The random nature of polio was cruel. I also knew that many children lacked the family supports I had. My father took on the job of in-home physical therapist. For years he worked with me to help stretch and strengthen the tendons and muscles that were having to compensate and substitute for those atrophied by polio. I was very surprised to learn later that I sometimes cried out in pain during those therapy sessions. I didn't remember the pain. What I remember was my dad's loving attention.

As time has passed, I have made a point of consciously reconnecting with "the polio years" in order to plan more effectively for my future as well as to more fully embrace my child self. As I age, I am giving up that prideful part of not wishing to acknowledge my limits and have instead begun practicing more intentional self-care. I now look back with compassion on my child self (as well as the many other children with polio, especially that child who cried inconsolably in the night). I have realized that withholding compassion for oneself translates into impaired compassion for others. Revisiting that period of my childhood has been an important threshold to cross.

A few months following my contraction of polio, the vaccine that could prevent polio was created. Forty-five years later, Phyllis and I brought our daughter to her pediatrician for her inoculations, including one for polio prevention. Perched on the bench, swinging her little legs, Noelle took the paper cup and calmly swallowed the oral vaccine. My eyes filled with tears, marveling at the miracle of protection she had received. Unknowingly, she had safely crossed a threshold.

In reflecting on these experiences, I recognize I am certainly not unique in the challenges of aging. My ninety-year-old neighbor is tethered to oxygen in her home until our icy winter passes and it is safer for her to go out again for limited periods with a portable tank. Mari is an avid reader with a razor-sharp mind, so our book exchanges and subsequent discussions are always stimulating. Spending time with her is like being shown cue cards for how to "sage" in place, lest I forget and merely age. Mari likes to keep magazine articles and newspaper columns on subjects she believes will (or should) interest her friends and then pulls them out and talks about them when we visit.

A British citizen who has lived in the US some sixty years, Mari offers vivid accounts of World War II and the London air raids, and what it was like to be a teenager living life behind blackout curtains. She is as interested in the world as she is proud of her great-grandson. Living with severe chronic obstructive pulmonary disease, her mobility is limited, but her mind travels far and wide. Recently, she pulled off a successful medical intervention for her ninety-two-year-old sister still living in the UK. In one of their daily phone visits, she suspected her sister was exhibiting signs of having had a light stroke. She kept her sister on the landline while she calmly dialed overseas emergency services on her cell phone and directed them to her sister's residence. After hospitalization, her sister is back home recovering, and their daily phone visits have resumed.

With regard to life's thresholds, I am taking as my inspirations our little grandson, my child self, and my ninety-year-old friend. From them, and in the loving company of my partner, I draw strength to boldly cross whatever threshold awaits me in this later chapter of my life, because I know I carry home with me. If I can continue to make home whenever I cross a new threshold or come home to the familiar comforts of an old one, I dare to believe I will "sage" in place and find home, wherever that is.

Tipping Points for Change

I had not planned on writing these next two chapters. I am compelled to write them, not because I am an expert on the subjects of gun violence and immigration, but because my conscience won't rest. I can't write about the universal longing for home as a place of safety, hospitality, and belonging while ignoring two key issues critically impacting children and youth in this country and at its borders: namely, our history with gun violence and our treatment of immigrants who are people of color seeking asylum in the US. These issues are not new, but they have gotten increasingly challenging and deserve serious conversation regarding how they reflect on the character and moral leadership of the United States of America. By the time this book is published, the statistics listed in these chapters will be outdated by ever increasing rates of violent and premature deaths. We ignore them at our peril, because how we respond—or fail to respond—to them will define us as individuals, as a country, and as citizens of the world.

While there have been horrifying mass killings throughout our country, those that involve the traumatization and deaths of children are particularly shocking. Who can forget the devastating murders of twenty children and six adults at Sandy Hook Elementary School in Newtown,

Connecticut, in 2012? Yet another massacre took place in 2018 at Stoneman Douglas High School in Parkland, Florida. Seventeen people were killed: two coaches and one teacher, as well as fourteen students. The gunman used a semiautomatic military-style gun, the weapon of choice for mass shooters.

The teacher who died was standing in the threshold to his classroom, quickly ushering in students from the hall to hide them. As the last one entered, this man was shot and killed blocking the door with his body while attempting to close and lock it. Because of his protective actions, that threshold provided a fragile opportunity for preserving the lives of the students who were hiding in the classroom. For the teacher trying to secure the door, that threshold became his point of departure from this world. I try to picture him falling into the waiting arms of love in another world. But that self-soothing picture in my mind is overcast by the shock of grief I know his family is experiencing from his murder in *this* world where they live.

In the days since the shootings, the students who survived this horror have been on the march. They have been joined by the now teenaged students from Sandy Hook, together with students in solidarity with them across the country. Together, they are calling out our politicians (all the way up to our chief executive) who have sold their will to enact effective gun safety legislation for money from the National Rifle Association to fund their elections. The Florida legislature has responded by fast-tracking the right of teachers to bear arms in school. What about fast-tracking the prohibition of semiautomatic weapons for nonmilitary use instead? Were the framers of the constitution really envisioning civilians armed with such weapons when their deadliest gun at the time was a single-shot musket?

It is telling that, despite what the Second Amendment says, not everyone *did* have the right to bear arms. Historically, Native Americans and African Americans were prohibited from owning guns. Constitutionalists feared that those disenfranchised populations in America could turn guns on their oppressors, though in fact, very few have. This is the hard truth of our history: the United States of America was settled by displacing native peoples from their ancestral homelands and then repeatedly violating treaties with them. "With the Removal Act of 1830 signed into law by President Andrew Jackson, tribes were persuaded, bribed and threatened off their lands." [21] When the Cherokee nation refused to leave, 16,000 were forcibly moved west by the US government in a brutal march remembered as the Trail of Tears. [22] It was a march essentially turned into genocide for the 4,000 Cherokees that did not survive hunger, disease, and the bitter winter conditions under which they traveled.

With land secured by the forced removal of First Nation peoples, American capitalism was then built from the human trafficking of kidnapped Africans and their subsequent enslavement to the cotton industry that benefited all the states, not simply Southern states. By 1860, "nearly four million American slaves were worth some $3.5 billion, making them the largest single financial asset in the entire US economy, worth more than all manufacturing and railroads combined." [23] It wasn't until the Thirteenth Amendment to the Constitution in 1865 that slavery was finally abolished. The hard truth is that "slavery made America." [24] To this day, the first century of our history casts a very long shadow over this "land of the free and the home of the brave." [25]

In our own time, "Black Americans are eight times more likely to be killed by firearms than those who are white." [26] It is shocking that "firearm homicide is the leading cause of death for African Americans between the ages of one and forty-four." [27] I write as one who benefits from white privilege, with some insight gained from having also experienced discrimination of a different sort. None of what I write is news to most First Nation peoples or African Americans. Imagine if these firearm homicide statistics were racially reversed. Inaction in Washington would be unthinkable.

In the previous chapter I talked about thresholds as passageways. But there is another meaning of threshold, which is to reach a point of saturation with something that signals a tipping point. While many adults are becoming numb to the culture of gun violence in America, the students across our country have reached their threshold for tolerance of elected officials who drag their feet on this issue because they are in the deep pockets of the NRA. These students are on the march, and as they become voting adults, I dare hope that we may be at a tipping point of change with respect to gun control. It is shameful, and at the same time encouraging, that our children are now leading us. Together, as they reach adulthood, we have the capacity to vote those politicians out who would risk young lives in exchange for NRA funding.

The students of Stoneman Douglas struggled to deal with the prospect of returning to the school where they hid, listening to gunshots around them while wondering if they would make it out alive. When discussing going back to school, one student survivor tried to comfort another with the words "It's still our home." Bravely spoken, yet how can it ever feel like a safe home after the carnage that took place there? Nonetheless, Stoneman Douglas students did go back to school, accompanied by their parents that first day.

Terry Spencer of the Associated Press described the event as follows:

> "They walked solemnly but resolutely Sunday through gates that had been locked to all but law enforcement and school officials since the Valentine's Day shooting, set to collect backpacks and other belongings left behind as they fled the massacre. . . . Junior Sebastian Pena said the gathering was a chance to see friends

> and his teachers, and to 'come together as a family.' The students were greeted by seventeen people dressed in white costumes as angels standing beside a makeshift memorial outside the school. Organizer Terry Decarlo said the costumes are sent to every mass shooting and disaster so the survivors 'know angels are looking over them and protecting them.' Many of those dressed as angels at Stoneman Douglas on Sunday were survivors of the 2016 mass shooting at the Orlando nightclub Pulse, where forty-nine people died." [28]

While I have been thinking about the thresholds that come with aging, a large segment of Americans are wondering if they and their children will even have a chance to age. When gun violence is the leading cause of death in Black one-year-olds, we have a crisis of belonging that leaves permanent scars among surviving family members as well as entire neighborhoods. To make homes with heart, we have to have safe neighborhoods.

Safety, hospitality, and belonging—the basic characteristics of what makes a house a home—should be universal. But that universality depends on racial and economic justice. We have repeatedly heard that, with respect to tax reform, "A rising tide lifts all boats." However, when economic policies benefit chiefly the top 1 percent of the population, private yachts just get bigger and bigger, swamping the little boats in their wake.

In Minnesota, we have plenty of gated communities. Wealth here is not splashy but discreetly hidden, like racism. The achievement gap within our educational system continues to grow as our educational models struggle to catch up to an increasingly diverse society. In my grandparents' day, it was a big deal for a Dane (my grandfather) to marry a Norwegian (my grandmother). The largely homogenous society of my youth has transformed relatively quickly into that of diverse cultures. Minnesota is beginning to make progress, but it will take more funding in education and more economic investment in African American and Native American communities as well as newer immigrant communities in order to shrink the gap in educational and economic achievement. The same may be said with respect to investing in affordable housing opportunities in all neighborhoods and racism training for safer policing in diverse communities. Our Twin Cities of Minneapolis and St. Paul are at a tipping point. Do we retrench or continue to invest in our diverse youth of today? Our hearts and minds and homes must expand to embrace our wonderfully expanding world.

Author's Note: Since this writing, another school shooting occurred on May 18, 2018, outside Galveston, Texas, with ten people killed and ten others wounded. [29] *CNN reports that from 2009–2018, there have been 180 school shootings on K–12 campuses and 356 victims. While Black students make up 15 percent of the more than 50 million students in the US, they account for about a third of the students who experienced a school shooting since 2009.* [30]

27

Families Seeking Refuge

In asking the question "What does home mean to you?" the responses I most frequently hear are, "a place of refuge where it's safe to be myself" and "a place I share with people I love." We can't be ourselves if our homes are not safe. Neither can we share who we are when we don't feel loved or valued. If family is "the climate that one comes home to," then our home is the place of refuge that shelters us amid life's storms.

Today, we are experiencing an international crisis of homelessness. For the influx of refugees fleeing war-torn countries, desperately seeking safe havens, home away from home has too often meant waiting in limbo in overcrowded refugee camps and temporary shelters in countries that do not want them. Historically, the US has welcomed refugees, chiefly of European origin. But we are now restricting immigration for people from mostly Muslim countries as well as from Latin American countries.

Since May of 2018, children accompanied by parents have been detained and then separated from their parents by order of the Trump administration. As of Independence Day, 2018, 2,600 children—some as young as babies—had been removed from their parents. A national outcry ensued, together with the initiation of a legal challenge to the order from the Democratic attorneys general in seventeen states and the District of Columbia. This resulted in a halt to the practice of separating families, followed by an order for reunification of families going forward. However, because of the haste with which they were separated, and some parents deported, confusion as to the whereabouts of parents and children has hampered reunification.

PBS NewsHour released a small sample of testimonies from parents and children who were directly impacted by the policy of separation. They have been released under the title "'My son is not the same': New testimony paints bleak picture of family separation." [31] The following are a few of their testimonies:

> "[My son] is not the same since we were reunited. I thought that because he was so young, he would not be traumatized by the experience, but he does not separate from me. He cries when he does not see me. That behavior is not normal. In El Salvador he would stay with his dad or my sister and not cry. Now he cries for fear of being left alone . . . when I took off his clothes, he was full of dirt and lice. It seemed like they had not bathed him the eighty-five days he was away from us."
>
> *~ Olivia Caceres, separated from her one-year-old son in November of 2018 at a legal point of entry. The boy's father, who was seeking asylum, remains detained.*

> "They told me to sign a consent form to take my daughter, but that it did not matter whether or not I signed, because they were going to take her either way." She further reported that officers at the border told her she would never see her daughter again and that she had "endangered" her by bringing her here. "I cannot express the pain and fear I felt at that point . . . One of the officers asked me, 'In Guatemala do they celebrate Mother's Day?' When I answered yes, he said, 'Then Happy Mother's Day'

because the next Sunday was Mother's Day. I lowered my head so that my daughter would not see the tears forming in my eyes. That particular act of cruelty astonished me then as it does now. I could not understand why they hated me so much or wanted to hurt me so much."

~ *Angelica Rebeca Gonzales-Garcia, apprehended and separated from her seven-year-old daughter in May of 2018.*

"My thoughts run in circles, and I feel as though I am going to lose my mind. I need to see my family and take care of them."

~ *"L. Doe," the father of a five-year-old son and an eighteen-month-old daughter, who wrote that he and his family presented themselves at a port of entry to apply for asylum. They were separated immediately.*

Unaccompanied minors from Latin America report fleeing gang violence, drug cartels, and economic insecurity as their main reasons for coming to the United States. Yet on June 20, 2018, Attorney General Jeff Sessions ruled that "the mere fact that a country may have problems effectively policing certain crimes—such as domestic violence or gang violence—or that certain populations are more likely to be victims of crime, cannot itself establish an asylum claim." [32]

We have severely narrowed the criteria for determining who can get asylum in the United States. We have split up families in the name of protectionism. We have denied detainees due process and have incarcerated them in facilities some of which are akin to those of convicted criminals. We have banned immigration and travel from Iran, Libya, Somalia, Syria, and Yemen, all majority Muslim countries. Currently, our country restricts and detains immigrants from Mexico, El Salvador, Guatemala, and Honduras, all of whose populations are majority people of color. While hundreds of children separated from their families have been released back to their detained parents under court order, thousands more who arrived as unaccompanied minors remain in detention in private shelters.

Over the years, we have had living among us children who were brought into this country illegally or who were born here since their parents' arrival. Now adults, these young "Dreamers" have grown up under the shadow of secrecy with no legal rights or protections. This is the country they have known and whose ideals beckoned to their parents. Yet, without a path to citizenship, they face the prospect of deportation to countries that they have never known or barely remember. Meanwhile, their future is held hostage to the political and racial divide in this country. The current administration is building a wall along our southern border. While border security is important, a wall must not be our country's chief response to today's immigrants who have been increasingly and unjustly cast as criminals who threaten our society.

Many among us believe there is a battle going on for the soul of America. But it is not too late to stop demonizing those perceived as "other." We can choose to write compassion into our national story instead of exclusion. The Evangelical Lutheran Church in America has seized this opportunity to lead with compassion. In response to the desperation of unaccompanied children and migrant families who are seeking refuge in the US at our southwest border, the ELCA has created the Guardian Angels initiative. This program provides trained, Spanish-speaking volunteers to accompany and guide new arrivals through their immigration court process. It also connects immigrants with resources for obtaining legal counsel and for transitioning to life in the US. With the participation of welcoming congregations, the ELCA is building community as "church together for the sake of the world." [33]

In all our disputes regarding immigration, we seem to have forgotten that the United States of America is a country founded by, and continually renewed by, immigrants. We are all indebted to those citizens whose ancestors were torn away from their tribal lands and their home countries. Their ancestors were the conscripted founders of this country. Our government received land by robbery and built a national economy through slavery. Two centuries ago, both Native Americans and African Americans had their children taken away from them. Native American children were forced to leave their communities to attend boarding schools designed to make them forget their families, their language, their land, and their spiritual heritage. African children born into slavery were pressed into service in white households and the fields of the cotton industry. Like livestock, they were continually subject to being resold and separated from their families at the whim of their white masters. This is our history. Moving forward, we need to ask ourselves, individually and as a nation: "Who have we become?" "Who do we want to be?" and finally, "How will we get there together?"

An editorial published in our local newspaper, the Minneapolis *Star Tribune*, eloquently imagines a new vision for our world and our country. Zaynab Abdi is an honor student at one of our universities. She is a legal immigrant who comes from war-torn Yemen. She writes: "My sister and I both applied for a visa to come to the United States, but her application was denied. Now, under the travel ban, my sister will never be allowed to come here . . . and I cannot leave to visit her because I may be banned from returning to my home in the United States. . . . I plan to finish my education and become a human rights lawyer to help other people who cannot finish their educations because of war or conflict or cultural barriers. . . . *I dream of a world where there is no war or violence, a world where there is peace and love. I dream of a world where newcomers are not seen as aliens or illegals, where we all see and celebrate our shared humanity, and families are able to live together.*" (Author's italics) [34]

We who are citizens of the United States are the agents of our own history, for good or ill. Moving forward, it will take all of us, and perhaps most especially our religious institutions, to make our history good. America's greatness lies in our graciousness. This country, and all its children, must become our common trust. I am reminded of something our daughter's preschool director said twenty-three years ago: "If we concentrated on meeting the needs of the world's children and taking care of Mother Earth, all our problems would evaporate, and we would become global citizens."

Her words are a reminder that I am obligated to those who rely on my voice, my vote, and my advocacy to support them in living safely in this, their country of refuge, regardless of how they got here. Let us all make America *gracious* again, and in the process, become citizens of the world. Let us make home—that place of safety, hospitality, and belonging—a universal human right!

Author's Note: Since this writing, the Evangelical Lutheran Church in America, a nearly 3.5 million member denomination, voted in 2019 to become America's first "sanctuary church body." Sanctuary means not only provision of shelter but also a response to raids, detentions, deportations, and the criminalization of immigrants and refugees. It includes strategies to fight individual cases of deportation and advocacy to end mass deportation. The ELCA believes it has "a moral imperative to take prophetic action of radical hospitality rooted in the ancient traditions of our faith communities." By doing so, the ELCA is determined to "demonstrate a vision for what communities and the world can be." [35]

Opening Home and Heart

Introduction: Rebecca and Esther's Family of the Heart

Rebecca and Esther are a couple who expanded their family through the practice of gracious hospitality extended to an immigrant mother and her baby during a time of great need. Esther is a social worker dedicated to justice work in fair housing. Her partner, Rebecca, is a music teacher.

RUTH: I want to begin by inviting you to tell your story of how you came to the decision to expand your family with a stranger and her baby. I will ask questions along the way as you tell it. But I want my questions to flow from your story so you can freely shape it.

ESTHER: Okay, I'll start. It began when our congregation was working on developing a sister parish tie with a congregation in Central America. A group of us from the United States went to Central America to meet with several congregations. While staying at a guesthouse, we met Hannah, who was another guest. While we stayed there, she confided her story to our little group.

REBECCA: Hannah had come from an African country where she had married a man of a different nationality. Because he was from the wrong tribe, both were considered to have violated the customs of their culture through their "intermarriage." A xenophobic mob that disapproved of their union came after them, viciously beating Hannah's husband unconscious. They then turned on her, and seeing she was pregnant, threatened to attack her and her unborn baby with machetes. Thankfully, they stopped short of this. As she fled for safety, Hannah didn't know if her husband was alive or dead. Much later she learned her husband had been hospitalized for months but had lived.

ESTHER: After the beating, Hannah was terrified, believing she and her unborn child were still targeted by this gang. With the help of a white family her mother worked for, Hannah obtained a plane ticket that would take her to Canada by way of a layover in Central America. Upon landing, Hannah gave birth to her baby boy during the layover and missed her connecting flight. She named her baby Matteo in honor of the kind stranger who delivered her baby.

REBECCA: Hannah and her baby were staying at the guesthouse convalescing. After learning her story, I wondered if I could help her seek asylum in the US. I had a contact with the US State Department in Hannah's home country and said I would talk to him. But nothing really came of that connection. Months went by, and we heard nothing from Hannah. Then we received a call from Hannah telling us she was in a detention center with her baby in a US border state. She had strapped her baby on her back and climbed mountains and crossed streams, aiming for Mexico. When they finally arrived in Mexico, Hannah and her baby were apprehended by border authorities. They were detained together. Hannah was now penniless and needed help.

ESTHER: Prior to our trip to Central America, we had been in the process of finding a new house. We had made an offer on this house that has more space than we really needed. While in Central America, we got a call from our realtor telling us our offer had been accepted. We wondered, "What are we going to do with this big house?" It was Rebecca who said, "What about helping a mother with a baby like Hannah and her son?" We returned home to the United States and moved into our new home. That's where we were, nine months later, when we got Hannah's call. It felt like God was delivering them to us.

RUTH: Were you at all concerned about how she might feel about living with a lesbian couple?

ESTHER: Yes, we let her know we were a couple, and she simply said she had had a gay friend in her home country. It wasn't an issue for her.

REBECCA: I think there were much bigger issues at stake that put that one into proper perspective. We all barely knew one another. Saying yes to this living situation demanded a lot of trust that it was meant to be. We could have said no to her request for help. The potential for it to turn into a disaster was certainly there, but the yes was so forcefully in our hearts we knew it was the right answer. And in retrospect, we've said many times, if Hannah hadn't been who she was, it really could have been difficult. Through all her extraordinary challenges—including suffering the effects of post-traumatic stress syndrome—Hannah was still incredibly resilient and determined to seek the best life for herself that would safeguard her son.

ESTHER: Once here, we knew she struggled with depression. She would withdraw for periods at a time and keep to herself. Matteo was delayed in his language and social development. It took him quite a while to gain enough confidence to explore his new world and trust this new living situation. I remember swinging him in one of those little bucket swings at the playground and realizing he was utterly terrified, just wordlessly enduring the experience until it was over. We realized we had to take things very slowly.

REBECCA: And it was also complicated by the fact that he didn't understand English, speaking only a little Spanish by the time he arrived here. So it all took time as well as patience. It was months before he could relax into play.

RUTH: You two created the safety and time he needed to gain that confidence.

ESTHER: Yes.

RUTH: What became of her husband?

ESTHER: He recovered, but it had been a new relationship, and they saw no way to be together safely. The relationship became unsustainable. They agreed to divorce for the sake of their child.

RUTH: Another difficult adjustment among many.

ESTHER: When she got here, we connected her to an organization that helps new immigrants with their English and helps them get an education.

REBECCA: When they first arrived, Matteo was totally hers. He was glued to her. And they lived pretty separately from us. But over time, they got more comfortable, and he became less scared. They both began spending more time downstairs with us, and after a while, she let us give her periods of needed respite by taking care of him. We started to become a real household by the end of the first year.

ESTHER: As he got bigger, Matteo was so much fun! He began romping around the house and playing games. But during this time, Hannah learned that her parents had died while she was making her terrible trek to get to the US. That sent her into a deep depression, and we knew we needed to be more of a presence for Matteo. It was a time when Hannah turned more to spiritual resources, reading the Bible for encouragement and comfort. And as it happened, I went through the deaths of my remaining siblings during that same time frame. So we were united in grieving together. Another of the benefits of this time is that it helped me heal more fully from my racist upbringing in the Deep South, just loving these two brown-skinned people.

RUTH: Can you expand a little on your familial connection to racism?

ESTHER: Yes. I had been doing some family research after my remaining sibling died. I traveled in the South to talk with my cousin who showed me some genealogical material she had. I found myself looking at this document she spread out before me. I stopped breathing, hoping against hope that it wasn't what it seemed—but it was. I held in my hands the original charter of the Ku Klux Klan in her family's southern city. My uncle was one of the signers of this document. It really took the wind out of me for a while.

Several months later, Matteo was baptized at the Easter Vigil. Our church's font, which held the baptismal water, was low to the ground so it was kid-friendly. Part of the liturgy included blowing on the water, symbolizing the baptism in the Spirit. So Matteo was right in there, blowing on the water of his baptism. I told the congregation, "It is only because of my baptism that I can claim another family, and it is why I work against racism. Because of what happens in baptism, we all take on the same unknowable, unspeakable last name of God. We all become family."

RUTH: A powerful image of grace. I know you also legally adopted Hannah. How did you come to that decision?

ESTHER: I had been walking the dog one cold winter day, and as I walked along, it was like God punched me in the ribs and in my mind I heard this voice saying, "You can adopt her." My immediate thought was, *You can adopt an adult? I didn't know that.*

REBECCA: (laughing) There was nothing planned out about any of this. It was just God unfolding events as we lived into them. As we talked it just seemed more and more that it would be a great thing to do.

ESTHER: We talked to Hannah about it to see what she thought, and she was surprised but moved by our proposal and agreed to the idea pretty easily. By then, we were all clear that adopting her would not affect her chances for citizenship, so it wasn't about that. The adoption was about making family, not about making a path to citizenship.

REBECCA: We didn't know we weren't quite complete until we lived into this. And I think you were grieving the loss of your family both from death and from discovering the hard truth of your genealogical roots in racism.

ESTHER: Yes, I was. It was grief at every turn because it also came at a time when our state was considering a constitutional amendment against gay marriage. It was just a hard time for gay couples. Then when we met with an attorney about the adoption, he wasn't very encouraging at all. After we left his office, and while we were waiting for the elevator, I just teared up and said to Rebecca, "Every time I love somebody, it's illegal."

RUTH: You just wanted to be a family together.

ESTHER: That's right.

RUTH: How great that you persisted and were ultimately successful in pressing for legal adoption.

ESTHER: We had such a sweet moment in family court. Hannah sort of paused in the proceedings, saying to the judge, "Your Honor, people don't often get an opportunity to have another mother. I just want to go on the record here about how honored and grateful I am to be part of this family."

REBECCA: Hannah and Matteo filled a void for us that we hadn't been aware of before they came into our lives. They just filled us up and filled us out as a family.

RUTH: It sounds like it fed your souls and eased heartache, especially with the addition of this child. You were having that rich experience of chosen family, what I call "family of the heart."

REBECCA: Yes, these have been life-changing years for all of us, especially the years they both lived with us. And now Hannah is remarried!

ESTHER: She's found a very good man. We're so glad for her new happiness with him.

RUTH: So if she is now married to an American citizen, will that permit her to stay in the US?

ESTHER: Not necessarily, especially in this social climate and under this administration. They want to be married two years before Hannah applies for citizenship.

RUTH: How is Matteo doing now?

ESTHER: Very well. He is excited to be studying music with Rebecca, who has been giving him lessons each week. He's learning about jazz because he wants to be a jazz trumpeter. He started out in beginning band and has graduated within a year to intermediate band.

RUTH: Spoken like a proud grandparent.

ESTHER: Yes, we are proud. Here, I can show you his picture. (We look at the picture of the bright-eyed boy with the winning smile while Esther continues speaking.) Rebecca has a cousin who has been working on the family tree and is making a document that updates it to show our expanded family in it. Matteo is very excited about that. He goes to all her family reunions. He can't wait for it to come. He's been going to them every year since he got here.

REBECCA: At our last reunion, someone asked where the next one would take place. My cousin said, "In Florida." After she left the table, Matteo started crying, and when I asked him why he was crying he said, "Because, if the reunion is in Florida, I won't be able to come." We assured him the family reunion wouldn't take place without him.

RUTH: Have the efforts of the Trump administration to limit applications for asylum together with the policy of separating children from parents increased uncertainty for Hannah and Matteo?

ESTHER: Oh, it has affected all of us terribly. But we have to take everything one day at a time and keep trusting that being family together has been part of God's intention for all of us.

RUTH: Earlier I wanted to ask you how your lives have changed since you opened your home and your hearts to Hannah and Matteo, but I think you've already answered that question.

REBECCA: As a couple, our conversation has shifted from "What's going on in our lives?" to "What's going on in our daughter's life and our grandson's life?" It takes us out of ourselves and into their best interests.

ESTHER: Just to say the words "my grandson" is life changing. I thought I would never say that. Then, "my daughter," and finally, "my son-in-law" . . . holy mackerel! I never thought I'd say those words. When I was feeling so bereft of family, God provided the funkiest family you could ever imagine! (She laughs.) I surely wouldn't have put this family together. From my KKK family of the South, through Africa and Central America to here, and now this adoption—it's just amazing.

REBECCA: It's a whole new perspective and a whole new life.

RUTH: And what a wonderful life it has become. I have so appreciated hearing your story. It seems especially important for it to be heard at this time in the life of our country. It gives us all hope. In my book I write about home as a place of refuge, hospitality, and belonging. You have brought all of that to a whole new level in the creation of this family. Your family of the heart story is an inspiration, and I'm glad many more people will get a chance to hear it. Thank you.

Going Home: Stories from Hospice

God's Way for Me

The profoundest thing
one can say of a river
is that it is on its way to the sea.
The deepest thought
one can think of persons
is that they are citizens of eternity.

Moments and years,
Years and moments,
pass like sea-bent streams.
And I? I'm carried on the current
of an all-possessing love.
I'm on my way, God's way for me,
so let it be.

~ Gerhard Emanuel Frost, *Seasons of a Lifetime*

Held in Blessing from Birth to Death

In the course of our lifetime, most of us experience several moves and several homes. Each one stretches us because it is the challenge of endings and the opportunity for new beginnings. Sometimes it results from plans we have made that have come to fruition, and other times it comes from loss and the need to regain one's footing somewhere else. The familiar saying "Bloom where you are planted" invites us to make an investment in each life setting whether we have chosen it or not. We know from gardening that transplanting always includes some shock to the root system that highlights the vulnerability of life. Nothing shocks the system more than to realize we are saying goodbye to all that we hold dear in this life. When death calls, what are the seeds of new life? Where will our little seed blow and take root? Who will tend this new life and welcome us home?

In the introduction to this book, I indicated that my work as a hospice chaplain has given me the opportunity to accompany many people as they prepared for and completed their passage from this world. They have been my teachers. What follows are some reflections on what I have learned about beginnings and endings from three sources. These sources are my hospice teachers, my roots in the Jewish/Christian tradition, and my study of the origins of two powerful words: "hello" and "goodbye."

I have come to believe that we humans do not *have* souls—we *are* souls. Put another way: "We are not human beings having a spiritual experience. We are spiritual beings having a human experience." [36] During our earthly sojourn, we all seek to make a home here because the longing for home is innate. It will never cease in this life. Perhaps it is given to us before birth and reaches its fulfillment after death when our souls leave our bodies behind in the exhalation of their last breath.

Our time in this world is very short even if we live to be ninety years old, and too many do not reach even nine years. Perhaps during our lifetime on this earth, everything truly worth doing and being will live on simply because it becomes part of the good millions of others bring to this world, known or unknown to us. What I know for certain is that whoever we have been and whatever we have done for the sake of love is our most important and most enduring legacy. Whether our individual lives here are remembered or forgotten, love ties us together.

In Hebrew Scripture, there are two complementary stories of the origins of creation presented in the Book of Genesis. The best-known story is in chapter one. It describes how God created the first humans, Adam and Eve, and entrusted them with the care of the earth. Many of us know how that turned out: paradise was lost through mistrust, shame, blame, greed, overreach, and bad stewardship. Sound familiar? It is an ancient story as apt today as it was centuries ago.

However, it is the second creation account that has spoken to me most powerfully in my work as a hospice chaplain. In this second chapter of Genesis, the Creator is shown gathering up some earth and fashioning it into an "earth creature" that just lies there, inert and inanimate. Then the divine creative presence does an astonishing thing. The Creator kneels over the lifeless form and breathes into its nostrils, and the creature slowly comes to life. In this account, the undifferentiated earth creature, *adam*, receives its name from the substance from which it is formed: *adamah*, which is the feminine form for "earth" in Hebrew. [37]

The next scene of the story shows the Creator responding to the loneliness of the earth creature *adam* by creating animals to inhabit the earth with it. That comfort fails to fully assuage the earth creature's loneliness, so the compassionate Creator casts *adam* into a deep sleep and reaches into the earth creature's side to fashion another corresponding creature from *adam*. With this new earth creature, the two are differentiated as male and female. *Adam* becomes male, and the new creature is introduced as female and named *Chava*, which in Hebrew means "mother of all life." In the Talmud, Eve was called Chava because she "nursed the whole world." [38] The English translation *Eve* downgrades the Hebrew meaning by rendering it simply as "life."

To contemporary ears, this image of creation calls to mind mouth-to-mouth resuscitation performed on a lifeless person in the hope that it will call them back from the edge of death. For a few minutes, their rescuer breathes for them, lending breath until they can breathe again on their own. This ancient creation account gives a picture of what human beings are: creatures of the earth who are animated by divine breath—the presence of spirit—within them. The word for spirit in Hebrew is *ruah*, which also means "breath" or "wind." [39] (This is similar to Christian Scripture, where the word for spirit in Greek is *pneuma*, which means "enlivening breath" or "wind.") [40] In this story from Hebrew Scripture—paralleled in the teachings of the Spirit in Christian Scripture, *humans share in divine breath*. Humans are creatures of the earth that are animated by the enlivening, indwelling presence of their Creator. In this life in this world, humanity is connected to the earth and all its life forms. We share common purpose: to love one another, to tend life, and to preserve space for all to thrive, whether we are life bearers or life stewards or both. If we accept this calling, it should inspire a high regard for one another, this earth, and our astonishingly intimate Creator.

This view of humanity has given me great respect for the process of dying, a process that takes our souls out of our bodies in death and returns our bodies to earth. The great mystery is: What happens to our consciousness after we die? Where does our breath go? My belief is that we are united in direct communion with the Sacred and all other sources of love that have gone before us or will arrive after us. This is congruent with the many accounts of near death experiences (NDEs) from those who have been declared clinically dead, only to be resuscitated or "sent back" to this earthly mode of life. It also resonates with my experience of being at the bedside of many people as they passed. I have witnessed them see and hear their dear ones coming to them. Often these presences appear to manifest themselves as guides for the way home. Most of us have had the experience of standing on sacred ground when being transfixed by a distant view. In the same way, we are privileged to stand on sacred ground as our loved ones pass from this life. The difference is, we are invited to trust the view *their* eyes see.

Working with families whose loved ones are on hospice means that when the end is near, the role of the chaplain is to support families in saying goodbye so they can release their loved one and ease their passage. My role with patients was to help them go peacefully through the power of blessing to release them from fear. In this process, knowing the origin of the words hello and goodbye can be very helpful to both patients and their families.

The greeting "hello" comes from the Old English word *hail*, which was a shout of praise or support. Derivations of hello in Spanish, German, and Classical Greek add the meanings "be well" and "good health." [41] "Goodbye" comes from *godbwye*, which is a contraction of the Old English blessing "God be with ye," often followed by "travel well." [42] This blessing was given in parting when people were dying (usually at home) or moving far away to distances beyond their loved ones' ability to travel.

Through the power of love, we are supported in our coming and our going by these two blessings: the one given to the newborn, "Hello, little one, *be well* and truly welcome," and that given to the dying one, "Goodbye, dear one, *God be with you*, travel well" (or alternatively, "Love be with you, travel well"). We come into this world to welcoming hands of joy at birth. We leave this earth with sending hands of blessing at death. When we allow these two blessings to hold the span of our lives, the burdens and sorrows of life are eased and our purpose and joy enriched.

Some people say, "I don't do goodbyes." This stems largely from fear that something bad will happen if goodbye is said or that it will hurt too much to say it to a loved one at time of death. When people understand the origin of goodbye as a blessing, it helps to take the sting out of it and remove fear. I have found that a simple "sending" ritual helps families say goodbye, giving families peace of mind and giving their loved one "traveling mercies" for their final journey.

During the ritual, families are invited to participate in anointing their loved ones with oil as a sign of love and blessing. Some use the sign of the cross. Others use a simple heart sign or a circle signifying the blessing of love that does not end. Each has an opportunity to bless their dying loved one in their own words, either aloud or in the silence of the heart. When they have finished, I close their blessings with a refrain from the song "Bread and Honey," by Canadian singer-songwriter Lowry Olafson. It was composed as Lowry reflected on the death of his own mother when he was still a young boy. I sing the refrain, adjusted when needed to reflect the gender of the patient, and set it to the more widely known hymn tune "The River Is Wide." The refrain of "Bread and Honey" is as follows:

"Fill this room with love and light,
Release her soul and give it flight,
Take her heart into your care,
And use our love to hold it there."

In the context of hospice, the ritual anointing with oil together with the words of Lowry's verse (sung or spoken) functions as a blessing before death. After death, it can be used as a commendation by changing "release her soul" to "receive her soul." The power of this blessing/commendation has been deeply appreciated by those who self-define as religious and by those who self-define more broadly as spiritual.

Phyllis continues to use this beautiful blessing/commendation with the families she serves on hospice, coupling it with accompaniment on her Reverie harp. Through our friendship with Lowry's sister Jan, we have had the honor of welcoming Lowry into our home to thank him in person for the power of his blessing. He has been touched to learn how much it has meant to the many people with whom we have shared it.

Lessons in Living from the Dying

No journey to find home around us and within us is complete without including some stories that come from end-of-life experiences. These stories speak to the power of blessing at end of life and pay tribute to the loving care extended by so many families as they see their loved ones off on their final journey home. My hospice teachers have included my parents, both of whom were on hospice before they died. In them, I have been blessed to have role models for how to live and how to die.

After my father's death in 1987, my mother spent her remaining years fiercely championing gay rights, becoming a force for change in her church community and in the seminary community. She became a friend and surrogate mother/grandmother to many gay and lesbian people who became her extended family, or "community of the heart."

In 1990, my mother flew out to San Francisco to attend our ordinations, accompanied by my sister Naomi. During the service, the congregation was invited to circle around Jeff, Phyllis, and me while we stood in their midst to receive a blessing. Somehow my mother saw to it that she and Naomi were positioned in the first ring of people that encircled us to lay their hands of blessing upon us. A press photographer captured this moment and later gave us a copy. To this day, it is a treasured memento of that occasion.

When Mother returned to Minnesota, she made a point of meeting with several key professors at the seminary where my father had taught for twenty-five years. Meeting one by one with them over tea in her home, she advocated for changes in church policy and within the seminary community. She stated that the moment had arrived to open the door to gay and lesbian people of faith who had long offered their time and talents to the church at all levels while living closeted lives. She urged her guests to seize the moment and use their influence to help make this happen. I learned this on one of my return visits when she spoke about it. When she ticked off the names of those professors with whom she had met, I asked curiously why a particular name had not been included on her list. Her quick response was, "Oh, Ruth Mary, he's weak. I don't bother with the weak ones!" Despite her deep grief in losing her beloved life partner, Mother had found her mission!

A decade later, my mother was diagnosed with idiopathic pulmonary fibrosis. As she lost much of her strength in her last months, she went out less and less, depending on her many years of diverse friendships to bring people to her. Every Friday, Mother received the Sacrament of Holy Communion from Bill, a gay man who directed her church choir and whose members sang for her shortly before death. At age ninety-one, Mother's last foray into the world came on Election Day. She was determined to cast her vote for the future she knew she would not see. Every election season, I remember Mother's investment in the common good and the effort it cost her. She makes me grateful for all our elders who help shape a future they care about for succeeding generations.

When my mother was just days away from death and residing in a residential hospice, my brother, John, recounts walking into her room and finding her sitting up in bed with a broad smile on her face. "Well?"

she asked. "Do you see her?" "See who, Mom?" my brother asked, looking around the empty room. Her face fell in disappointment and she replied, "Oh, you can't see her then. It's my sister Dorothy. She's here. My mother is here too. They're waiting for me." Cautiously, my brother asked, "Is Dad here too?" "No," she replied, calmly. "Gerhard has been content to keep himself hidden."

As I reflect on this from my vantage point working in hospice, it is striking to me that my mother's apparent "guide" was her deceased younger sister, who had been troubled by addiction and alcoholism throughout her life and with whom my mother had a loving but strained relationship. I believe the strain between the sisters was largely due to my mother having led a much more fulfilling life with my father than Dorothy had been able to have with her two husbands, both alcoholics. My father, who had added stability coupled with deep love for my mother, was described as "content to keep himself hidden." I like to believe he was in the background, patiently waiting his turn, glad to be able to support my mother in her reunion with her departed sister and happy to let sister and mother welcome her first. That belief is in keeping with his nature. He was a gracious man.

At Mother's funeral, I shook hands with scores of gay and lesbian people who were eager to tell me how much my mother had meant to them and how strongly she had encouraged them. I also shook hands with the former bishop of her district who spoke of what a remarkable woman she was. He told me she had met with him to urge him to follow his heart and exercise greater leadership for changes in church policy regarding the full recognition of gay and lesbian people in all facets of ministry. He then confessed with a chuckle that she had asked him pointedly, "You're in your second term of office, so you're not running for reelection. What's holding you back? Is your wife holding you back?" His wife, who was standing next to him as he gave this account, leaned toward me with a wry smile and interjected, "Ruth, I *wasn't* holding him back!"

After that conversation with my mother, this former bishop did indeed become a leading voice for change. A few years later, he officiated at the "extraordinary" ordination of Anita C. Hill, a pioneer in her own right through Wingspan Ministry in St. Paul, Minnesota. Phyllis and I had been beneficiaries of Anita's earlier groundbreaking work on behalf of LGBT people in the ELCA and were delighted to celebrate her ordination as she had celebrated ours. Mother's memorial gave me a window into the scope of her own ministry of advocacy as well as those she had touched.

Back at Mother's house after the memorial, I paged through her hymnal still resting on the table by the chair where she had spent most of her last weeks after she lacked the energy to leave her home. Having no longer enough breath to sing, Mother had simply read through the hymns, prayers, and psalms. She had scrawled notes in the margins of the hymnal and underlined psalms and prayers that were particularly meaningful to her. However, my attention was drawn to a sheet of paper tucked into the hymnal. On it she had written two columns. The left-hand column was titled, "What I have received this week," and the right-hand column read, "Gifts to be given."

The left-hand column contained these items: "The cardinal singing at my window today, visits from hospice, listening to Bach, letter from Naomi, Paul (her Jewish neighbor) reading the Psalms to me, visits from Rosie and Mattie" (my brother's golden retrievers). In the right-hand column she had listed: "Check to LLGM, tithe to church, book for Lois (a member of her book club), piano music for Bill, phone call to Natalie after her surgery, thank-you note to Mike" (her congregation's custodian who kept the bathrooms immaculate).

The legacy my mother left in that list, made as she was in the slow but inexorable process of dying, is precious. It is a prescription for living a good life. In all things, however small, be mindful of the gift given. Under all circumstances, however difficult, keep giving. The first will renew your joy, and the second will save you from despair.

Five years after my mother's passing, my sister Miriam was diagnosed with late-stage breast cancer that had metastasized throughout her body. Only a few years earlier, Miriam had nursed her husband in their home while he was on hospice until his death. In my last visit to her, I saw that she was in a great deal of pain. We discussed how choosing comfort care through hospice could provide better pain management. But she was not yet ready for that option. She continued to press on with treatment and, on the advice of a surgeon, even consented to surgery on her hip. Because cancer had invaded her bones more acutely than any of us had fully realized, the surgery only added to her pain and accelerated her decline. However, it was clear that her motivation to fight on stemmed from hoping she could be mobile again and have more time with Rachel, her only child.

Following surgery, Miriam was in a continuously agitated state coupled with increased pain. Despite our requests for better pain management, her pain, agitation, and disorientation persisted. It was mid-December, and holiday decorations festooned the hospital floors. One evening while her daughter was also present, I simply sang Christmas carols I knew were familiar to both of them. As Rachel joined in and the two of us were singing, we heard a beautiful voice fill in the alto parts. It was Miriam, still in pain and half "out of it" but rising to the occasion. While singing, she appeared to be blessedly suspended in a state of peace. One of her nurses paused in the doorway, utterly amazed by what she was hearing, transfixed by the calm beauty of Miriam's voice as we all sang "Silent Night" together.

I have sheltered that moment in a protective place in my memory, because in the days that followed, she reverted to her state of unremitting agitation and discomfort. I also knew I needed to return to Minnesota to see our daughter dance in an important school production. There was no real "goodbye" in my last day with Miriam because she wasn't able to be present enough to hear my goodbye through her agitation. It was a terrible time to walk away.

Two weeks later, back in Minnesota, I received a call letting me know that Miriam was on the palliative care unit of the hospital. She was now close to death and unable to speak. I asked for the phone to be held to her ear so I could send my love and say goodbye. I could tell that she heard me by the change in her breathing as it slowed. That night, which was New Year's Eve, I went to bed with a heavy heart, but with relief that her pain and agitation were now well managed under palliative care. I awoke in the dark around four o'clock to beautiful music lingering in my mind from my dream state. It was the closing line from the carol "Away in a Manger." Over and over I kept hearing, "Bless all the dear children in thy tender care, and take us to heaven to live with thee there." In my heart, I knew Miriam was leaving. I woke Phyllis to tell her, "I think Miriam is going." That morning, I got the call that gave me the news I already knew. Miriam had died on New Year's Day, having paused to say her own goodbye to me as she went on her way.

That holiday will forever be a holy day to me. While I miss her, I never dread celebrating New Year's Day because I know Miriam's suffering mercifully and peacefully ended in the loving arms of Rachel, the one dearest to her. I cannot think of a more appropriate day for leave-taking and the embrace of a whole new life. Thanks to my work in hospice, I know that none of my loved ones who have passed on are lost to me. In truth, I believe our loved ones know and love us and send us their blessings from the vantage point of their best selves and their deepest healing. I know that none of us need be stuck in our worst moments of this life.

While we can learn from them, we don't need to keep living them because our loved ones certainly aren't. We are loved and forgiven unconditionally right here in this moment. And forever "hereafter."

Meeting Heart to Heart When Memory Fades

When I was a young adult, I avoided visiting nursing homes because I thought the environment in most of them was frightfully depressing. As a result, I carry with me a deep regret that I did not visit a beloved aunt after she went into a nursing home in a town a couple of hours distant from ours. Fortunately, she had nieces and nephews in that area who extended love and care to her in her remaining years. As a result, they got to enjoy a well-deserved special relationship with her in her old age, a relationship I missed out on because of my inhibiting fear. Going into ministry and later becoming a hospice chaplain released me from that fear and, to some extent, enabled me to make amends vicariously by truly being there for other elders.

Among the elders I visited, the one population among them I still felt uneasy with were those who suffered from dementia, the imprisonment of the diseased brain to failing memory. I wondered how two minds could meet under those circumstances until I realized it wasn't the meeting of minds that mattered but rather the meeting of hearts. I also learned that if the patient can still speak, some long-term memories are still accessible and can be shared, even though present time leaks away. The key is to be present to people with dementia in whatever time you find them and by any means they enjoy. My patients with dementia became some of my most valuable teachers. The following are a few examples:

ARNIE

This was my first visit with Arnie, who seldom spoke, according to the staff. I was told Arnie liked to sit for hours at a time at the end of the hall where someone had built a model of a car dashboard with a bench car seat. This was placed directly in front of a low window where you could look out while "driving." A nurse informed me that on good days, Arnie could track well enough to engage in very simple conversation.

Arnie was sitting in his "car" gazing absently out the window when I approached. I introduced myself and asked if he was about to go for a ride. He nodded an affirmative. I asked where he likes to drive. "In the country," he replied. I told him I loved the country too and asked if I might join him on the ride. He nodded and said, "Sure," patting the "car seat." For the next twenty minutes we "drove" in the country together (with Arnie at the wheel smiling). It was clear that he had grown up on a farm, because farm animals and crops featured quite often in what he was seeing and pointing at. I noticed his mood became increasingly upbeat. At the end, I thanked him for the ride, and as he opened my invisible door for me, he said, "Anytime!" That was the beginning of many rides together.

Arnie allowed me to practice meeting people with dementia where they are by graciously inviting me into his early life history. And I gave him a chance to enjoy company as he relived the freedom of driving and a happier time.

DOLORES

Dolores was completely nonverbal and wheelchair bound. She was physically and emotionally "locked in." As a result, it was difficult to tell how much Dolores could comprehend. Sometimes I sang to her, mostly hymns that I knew she had heard in church as a child, because music soothed her. One winter day, I found Dolores alone in her room sitting in her wheelchair facing the wall. The lights were off and the curtains closed. She was awake and motionless. I greeted her and told her it was a beautiful winter day and the snow was falling. I invited her to watch it fall with me. There was no reply or change of expression. I opened the curtains and gently turned her chair to face the window. I drew another chair close to hers. We sat, side by side, in silence, watching the snowfall. Then she gave a deep sigh and, still looking out the window, leaned her head against mine. After a while I said, "Dolores, you are much more than you can tell me. But God knows all of you and loves you. God has not forgotten you." At that, silent tears coursed down her cheeks. We sat, head to head, until an aide came to take her to supper.

Dolores taught me the power of presence in the midst of loss. She also taught me to enter her desolation and abide there with her before offering reassurance of her value to God.

ELIZABETH

Elizabeth was the most challenging person with dementia I regularly visited. This was because she had suffered severe abuse in childhood. With dementia trapping her in exclusively long-term, childhood memories, the abuse became an incessant reliving of trauma. It was amplified by her repeated efforts to save a younger sibling from becoming another victim of her abuser. She could get mental respite when she was awake and participating in a group situation that focused on a simple activity. But when she lay down to sleep, the family nightmare would take her back and hold her in its grip. Over and over, she would relive the struggle to flee with her sister to a place of safety.

In consultation with my hospice team, the nursing home staff, and Elizabeth's daughter (Elizabeth's sister was no longer living), we decided to try a variety of integrative medicine therapies. In addition to medication, we used guided meditation along with music therapy and essential oils in an effort to relieve some of Elizabeth's emotional suffering. I scheduled my visits in the afternoons when Elizabeth would be due for an afternoon nap. These became spiritually guided meditation times with the goal of providing Elizabeth a place of mental safety and emotional respite as well as sleep. Taking a cue from *The Lion, the Witch and the Wardrobe* by C. S. Lewis, I used the device of the magic wardrobe through which the children discovered the land of Narnia. For Elizabeth, Narnia became a safe place where she and her sister could hide and Elizabeth could get respite from memories of abuse. These combined resources helped Elizabeth relax into sleep. They were not a cure, but they provided temporary respite and a place of sanctuary for a tormented mind.

Elizabeth taught me how the struggle to find home and experience it as sanctuary can be so difficult for those whose childhood experiences of home were defined by abuse instead of nurture. It was heartbreaking to see the struggle magnified through dementia. But our team rejoiced in the small mercy of episodic relief Elizabeth received.

ANNETTE

A socially skilled woman who suffered from dementia but could still enjoy conversation, Annette could recognize my face after several visits without ever remembering how she knew me. I found that simply saying, "I know your daughter" (which was true because her daughter and I had several visits separately) was enough to relieve her anxiety about not remembering who I was from visit to visit.

One day, Annette initiated what became a more substantive conversation. She asked me, "What's going on in your life?" We talked a bit, she frequently losing the thread of the conversation but clearly engaged in the visit. Then, out of the blue she said, "I want to ask you something." Encouraged to go ahead, she said, "Well, you know I'm not religious. I mean, I believe in God, but . . ." Her voice trailed off. I replied, "Many people find God in places outside of church." Annette nodded and continued, "How do we know God is . . . God is . . . " She trailed off again. "Are you asking how we know God is really here with us?" I wondered. "Yes!" she replied emphatically.

I responded, "I think anytime we open our hearts to love, God is right here in that love." "That's something!" she replied. I continued, "God is here when we love our children." "Yes!" she replied. "And God is there when someone is kind to us," I said. "We can't see God, but we can see love. God is in the love." "You've got it!" she exclaimed with excitement. After a pause she asked, "Do you think the world knows?" "Well, I think the world tries to know, but sometimes people lose hope when they go through hard times and the world is cruel to them." "We need to tell them!" Annette replied. I asked, "Should we pray for the world and tell the world in our prayer today how much God loves them?" Annette nodded and folded her hands immediately.

We held hands, and I gave thanks for the gift of love in our lives and prayed for people who were sick or going through hard times. Then I prayed for Annette and the people on her floor and for her daughter. Afterward, Annette said thoughtfully, "There's more than this world." She leaned forward and added in a conspiratorial whisper, "*There's something dancing out there.*"

Annette died three weeks later. She reminded me that people with dementia are still spiritual beings even in the midst of being mentally compromised.

Cultivating a Vibrant Spiritual Life

As I look back on my life in ministry, I am deeply grateful for the spiritual gifts I have received. I am indebted to all those who have pioneered the way for me, to loved ones who have supported me through significant life changes, to a visionary congregation that practiced compassion as well as a passion for justice, and to those hospice patients and families who opened the curtain on their lives for me. Their wisdom has enriched me, guided me, and nurtured hope. Now as I begin my "third act," I see that all along the way, even in the worst times, my life has been illumined by grace.

From my work in hospice with people who have been marginalized by church and society, I have found that increasingly people are identifying with spirituality more readily than with religion. In elders, this is usually the result of some kind of negative experience with a specific community, its clergy, or its polity. Among younger adults, it is more commonly simply a case of having grown up with more diversity and a looser affiliation with religion. As a result, they are not hesitant to be eclectic and cross-cultural in their spiritual formation. The bottom line is that people, both young and old, are identifying as spiritual instead of religious because it allows them to be more authentic and gives them "breathing room." This has led me to ponder, "What does it mean to be spiritual?"

I have come to understand spirituality as a way of thinking and living that calls on deep love, encourages healing, and promotes peace. Love and blessing transcend religious creeds and are available to everyone. Spirituality has many expressions and many cultural influences, but at its loving core, spirituality is grace, gratitude, and gift. It is both personal and communal. There are no insiders and no outsiders, no chosen and no un-chosen. We are all one. We are all deeply connected to each other regardless of our life circumstances. This applies not only to humanity but includes the web of all life. We are to live in this world not as entitled conquerors but as humble guardians, taking care to protect and serve this earth that is home to all its creatures.

I believe that spirituality is not the antithesis of religion but rather its openhearted center. When a religion loses spirituality, it has lost its heart, and terrible things are then said and done in the name of that religion and its corrupted deity. So the question asked by many who have seen that corruption is, "Can you be spiritual without being religious?" I believe you can. The next question that begs to be asked is, "Can you be religious without being spiritual?" I do not think so. Spirituality can thrive without religion, but religion cannot thrive without spirituality.

Deepening our spiritual life depends on cultivating habits of kindness, gratitude, and grace. How would it change us to live as though we are all universally and equally connected, to live as though life is an unearned gift, and to live with the conviction that nothing good is truly lost? The Golden Rule, "Do unto others as you would have them do unto you," is the common heart of both spirituality and religion. There is a saying: "Not all of us can do great things. But we can do small things with great love." [43] However, when we collectively do small things with great love, we dare trust they will yield great results.

As physical powers diminish with age and we face life-limiting disease, we are invited to shift our focus from *doing* to *being*. This is a time of great vulnerability and even greater opportunity for us. Even when we are less able-bodied, we still have the ability to do small things: a word of thanks to a caregiver, a smile, an empathic recognition of another's burden, the silent holding of a hand, or a prayer from the heart. In this process, we *become* the blessing to those around us. On more than one occasion, I have had an adult child of a parent who has required total care near the end of life say, "When I came into the world, I required total care, and Mother provided for my needs. Now it's my turn to provide for hers." The rhythm of giving and receiving is dynamic and always intertwined, because that's how it's supposed to be. In our elder years, the most important gift we have is the gift we have *become,* because of how we have lived and how we have been loved. Our legacy is love; the gift is grace.

Now a retired chaplain, I draw on the blessings of all my spiritual guides to fully mine this "third act" of my life. When this act comes to a close, I will look again to those who have gone before me to guide me home. In their leave-taking, they have opened a portal through which to glimpse eternity. While awaiting my departure, I can think of no better accompaniment than music and those I love to see me off (and, if it's allowed, a dog). Just as we "make home" wherever we are, so we also must be ready to travel when it is time to leave this home for another.

Having been the beneficiary of much wisdom, I feel it is only right to share it. I offer the following keys to finding a vibrant spiritual life, courtesy of those who have gone before me and those who still accompany me, together with some insight of my own:

1. Regard life as a sacred gift and mortality as the means by which we appreciate it.

We sing our life song from our first cry to our last sigh. If we all share divine breath at birth and release our last breath in death, I trust we awaken as spirit to a new dawn, becoming fully alive in the oneness of our being with all life. My prayer is that each life song shall be woven into and transformed by the healing music of our collective voice, releasing sorrow into joy.

2. Choose to become an authentic human being living in harmony with your values.

Speak the truth of your experience. To loved ones, speak the truth with love. To those in power, speak the truth with courage. To those who are afraid, speak the truth with compassion. If we listen from our heart to the experiences of others, they will speak from the heart. We must strive to be transparent to ourselves and to others so that our inner and outer selves are in harmony. Live in tune with your core values but save some bending room. Trees need space to sway in order to thrive, and so do people. We easily praise people for having the courage of their convictions. But we seldom praise those who have the courage to change their convictions when they realize they were held at the expense of other people. Many violent acts have been carried out in the name of a conviction. Our convictions are seldom completely pure. They require reexamination throughout life.

3. Create homes with heart and families of the heart wherever you live.

Turn living spaces into loving places by cultivating families of the heart and drawing upon community wherever you live. Choose families wisely and be open to being chosen. Practice hospitality. When we participate in what unites us here on earth instead of what divides us, we glimpse heaven.

4. Ask the hard questions but trust the mystery.

Both questioning and trusting are necessary to lead us into deeper meanings, and ultimately to what or who we name as sacred. Ask questions in good company, and you will gain relationship if not answers. Eventually, we may learn to trust a greater Wisdom more than needing all our questions answered.

5. Live time. Don't just mark time.

Time is a gift too precious to waste. Be conscious enough of time to notice its passing. Savor the moment—it's where we are supposed to live. Equally, engage in life fully enough that there are periods when you forget the passage of time. Ask yourself, *What am I doing, and with whom, when I lose all track of time?* Does the answer bring you joy?

6. Count your blessings so you can be a blessing.

Cultivate and practice the daily habit of gratitude and the expression of affirmation as well as appreciation. Do it with strangers as well as loved ones. Give back what you can; pay forward what you can't.

7. Work for justice and build bridges toward reconciliation.

Accept the fact that you won't get through life without being hurt and without hurting others. Seek forgiveness and be willing to forgive yourself. Forgiveness allows failure to become a learning experience. Becoming mired in hatred or numbed by indifference is a dangerous waste of time. Both constrict the heart and stunt insight needed for growth and change. We are all complicit in some form of wrongdoing, but we cannot let this paralyze us into doing nothing. Let us work to make our world a better home for everyone. "Strong people stand up for themselves. The strongest people stand up for others." [44]

8. Take time to pray or meditate daily.

Prayer and meditation is available to us all. As our bodies have the power to make love, so our spirits have the power to create healing. Prayer and meditation is listening to and abiding in a power that flows through us and is intimately connected to us. At any time, we can draw on that power that dwells within us and among us. The writer Anne Lamott identifies three essential prayers for spiritual growth and practice that she uses as a title for one of her inspiring books, *Help, Thanks, Wow*. If I could make one addition to those three important prayers, it would be "Sorry." With "sorry," we begin the path to forgiveness; "help" assures us we need not make our way alone; "thanks" invites us to live in gratitude; and "wow" teaches us to be wonderstruck.

9. Expect to suffer and use it as a resource for compassion.

Years ago I heard of a woman who had suffered a brain aneurism. She survived with some cognitive impairment. A close friend asked her, "Do you have any sense of why this happened to you?" She replied, "Oh, I don't think we can ever know such things. We can only learn to make them count." For me, these have been words to live by and better than any of the convoluted or simplistic efforts to explain away or ennoble suffering. If left to our own devices, would we ever choose anything that could hurt us? Even apart from random catastrophic events such as a brain aneurism, the truth is, most things that could be regarded as worthwhile will stretch us beyond our comfort zone. Salvation can sometimes take the form of rescue from a perilous situation. But mostly, salvation (wholeness) is healing balm—salve for the inevitability of life's wounds.

10. Trust in grace.

Life is a gift to be received and fully lived. Grace is our "traveling mercy" for the road. It comes in pace with need, not in advance of it. "Grace meets us where we are but does not leave us where it found us." [45]

11. Commit to love: Love has both traveling power and staying power.

While we can't always be cured of what afflicts us, we *can* experience the healing, renewing power of love on our hearts and spirits. We can afford to live and love fully, because love is never a zero-sum game. It exists to be given away, without ever being used up. Love is the best companion in time of sorrow. It is also what unites us with those who have gone home before us and renews us to commit to those who still dwell among us.

12.Live in forgiveness.

"Live in forgiveness, claim your wholeness, and go in peace." [46] What better way is there to live this life and, eventually, leave it? Love invites us to live wholly so that we may die whole.

Life is dynamic, always in motion. It is the change agent for which we can never be fully prepared. But for those of us who are privileged to live the full arc of our lives into our elder years, there is great richness to the past because it reveals our life's meaning over time. From it we draw courage and strength to take the last leg of our journey in this world that will carry us across the threshold of eternity.

However long we live, the purpose of this life may be summed up as follows: to cherish the earth and all its creatures, to discover our gifts in order to give them away, to delight in the gifts we receive from others, and to give thanks for the gift of life itself. In my third act, this is the essence of my learning and my conviction: *Home is ultimately a spiritual journey, in good company. The way home is love. Our destination is our beginning, the Lover of us all.*

Marked by Love

"We have a man who is dying, and his family is asking for a chaplain. He's being cared for at his son's home. Can you come?" asked the on-call nurse late one night. As I drove to the house in an outlying rural area, I repeated the prayer I always pray: "God, help me to be an instrument of your grace and comfort for this patient and his family." Forty-five minutes later, I stood outside a farmhouse under a starlit sky and rang their bell.

Inside the house, I was greeted by a family of ten people and led to the bedside of an elderly man who was lying in the living room, surrounded by all his loved ones. His wife, his adult children together with their spouses, and his four grandchildren under the age of eight were all keeping vigil with their now unresponsive loved one. After introductions, I asked if one of them would be willing to tell me a story that would help me picture what he was like before he became ill. The children responded first, telling me all about how "Grandpa Tim" loved to watch bull riding and used to take them to rodeos. They also said that whenever Grandpa visited, he always brought their favorite treat with him, a box of Krispy Kreme donuts to pass around to everyone. This was Grandpa's last visit, they said, for he had come home to die.

"Grandpa's so sick he can't talk to us anymore," said the littlest one.

"That's right," I said. "He can't talk anymore now because he's getting ready to take a long journey where we can't follow. His body is tired out, and he will soon stop breathing. When that happens, his spirit will leave his body behind and go home to God." "Is his spirit like a good ghost?" asked one child. "Well," I replied, "we all have spirit inside us. Our spirit is that part in each of us that knows how to love. That part of us never dies. Your grandpa's love for you and yours for him will always be with you. You can hold onto it forever. But I think we can help your grandpa on his journey by giving him a blessing." "What's a blessing?" they asked. "A blessing is another way to give someone hugs and kisses before they have to leave us. It's a way of giving them love they can take with them. Would you like to give Grandpa Tim some love for his journey?" "Yes, yes!" they all chorused.

I took out my phial of oil and opened it up and held it so all the children and adults could see it. "This is olive oil that has been blessed," I said. "In our homes we use it for cooking. But long ago, when someone got hurt, people used it for treating wounds for healing too. They called it the 'oil of gladness.' We're going to use it to mark Grandpa Tim with our love, so that the sadness in his heart over leaving all of you will be comforted by your love. You can mark him on his hands or his forehead or anywhere you wish, and when you mark him, you will be giving him your love to take with him to keep forever. If you want to, you can say something out loud when you mark him, or you can just love him quietly in your heart. He'll know, either way, because he knows you by heart, even though he can't talk anymore."

Oil passed from child to child, and from adult to adult, and Tim was marked with love forever. Private tears and whispered words accompanied this ritual. As little hands patted his face and marked his forehead, Tim turned his head away from the wall and toward his family. When we were all finished and I had said a prayer and given Tim a final blessing, the littlest grandchild piped up, "Can we do this again?" "No, honey," his mother replied. "Grandpa has all the love he can carry now. He doesn't need anymore. His arms are full.""*I* know," cried the oldest child. "There's one more thing we *can* do," and with that he disappeared into the kitchen, reemerging carrying a box. Opening it, he began passing out its contents. That night, we shared another sacrament, the sacrament of love symbolized in the breaking and sharing of Krispy Kreme doughnuts all around. Twenty minutes later, Tim died, taking with him all the love he could carry and leaving us filled with love forever.

Brian's Journey Home

I made my initial spiritual care visit and met with Brian, his wife, Cathy, and the couple's thirteen- and fourteen-year-old sons, Jonathan and David. We had a lengthy discussion of family concerns. Brian talked about what it had been like for him when his own father died when Brian was twelve years old. He recalled feeling very angry about his dad's death and feeling so guilty about his anger that he kept it a secret from his mother. He said he started acting out in ways that were destructive. He worried that his sons would be angry with him for dying early in their lives and was concerned what that could lead to.

We talked about how everyone deals with grief in their own way and that no way is right or wrong, that many different feelings are part of the grief process. I pointed out that he was making it possible for his sons not to feel ashamed of their feelings by talking about his. Brian replied, "I don't want my boys to have to hide anything and feel bad about what they've hidden." His sons assured him they would talk when they needed to. "But who will we talk to when Dad's gone, and Mom has her own grief to deal with?" Jonathan wondered. "Who would you want to talk to?" his father asked. The boys thought for a moment and then identified their uncle Eddie, their father's brother, as the one they would want to talk to when their mom wasn't available. They both agreed that they would ask Uncle Eddie if he would be willing to be their confidant when they needed one.

"What do you most want to do as a family with the time remaining to you?" I asked.

Brian replied immediately, "Watch movies at home, have popcorn, fish with my boys . . ." After a pause, he added, "And then keep a date with my wife and go to Paris. It's been a long-standing dream. We have to do it soon while I can still get around. Can you help us with some hospice contacts while we're over there? Even if my cancer forces me to stay behind in the hotel most of the time, I can still join them for dinner, hear their stories of what they saw. I want my family to have something they'll always remember." Hearing about Brian's dream, a friend who owned a vacation timeshare arranged for time in Paris and then donated it to Brian's family, arranging for friends in Paris to host the family on a boat tour of the city. Our hospice social worker supplied hospice contacts abroad should they be needed. And so it was all arranged.

When Brian and his family returned from their trip, Brian admitted that once there, he did have to stay behind to rest most of the time. But he wasn't alone. His son Jonathan stayed behind with him, enjoying his father's company. I could see that Brian's energy had been drained by this trip but that it had been well worth it to him. Brian readily talked about his own death now. He said he had dreamed he was dying and had awakened gasping for breath. "I don't want to die that way—in pain and gasping for air." I assured him we had medications to help relax his breathing and keep him comfortable when the time came. I asked him what he needed emotionally in order to die peacefully, and he replied, "No pain. My wife's hand in mine, the boys as near as they want to be without having to feel afraid, and my extended family close by as support for Cathy." I suggested we share his wishes with his family and pray for this, trusting that God and his family would hear the longing of his heart, and we did so. Brian was tearful but less anxious.

Then he admitted that he had some fears that he had not been a "good enough" person in the past to merit God's love. I reminded him that Scripture is filled with seriously flawed individuals whom God chose to use as leaders in their spiritual communities, and then I gave him some examples of their nefarious personal histories. Brian listened and smiled, remarking, "Well, you've taken care of *that* fear! And I've said my confession, and the priest told me that as confessions go, it was pretty boring. But I'm holding on to what you said last time. Remember? You said, 'Our destination doesn't depend on how good *we* have been, but on how good God is.'" He then added that his boys had already become young men in this process of dealing with their father's end-of-life journey, and that he knew they would be okay.

Brian turned to his wife and said, "I heard a voice this morning asking me if I was ready. I thought at first that it was you just asking me if I was ready to get up. Then I realized it wasn't you. And I had to stop for a moment and think if I am ready. And I realized I think I am." With tears in her eyes, Cathy leaned toward him, took his hand, and said, "I want you to know that I'm ready to let you go whenever you need to."

A few days later, Brian's condition changed, and Cathy knew the end was near. She asked me to meet separately with each of the boys to get a sense of how they were doing. I did so, and in those conversations, I asked each of them the same question: "What have you learned by accompanying your father in his journey this far?" David replied, "I've learned a lot from Dad being sick. Sometimes people have to become older quicker than they expected. I'm becoming older now. When Dad dies, Mom will be a single parent, and I will be helping her by doing some of the things Dad usually did. I've asked Uncle Eddie to teach me how to use Dad's tools."

When I asked the question of Jonathan, he thought for a moment and then said, "When I can't sleep at night, that's when my thoughts come. I don't think anything worse could happen than Dad dying. But I've learned that even when the worst happens, there's good stuff in it too. We're all closer. We talk about everything now. In Paris, my favorite time was when I stayed with Dad at the timeshare, and we just talked."

I reported to Cathy that she didn't need to be anxious for her sons. Even though they would grieve deeply, they would still be okay. Cathy was relieved. She commented, "I'm juggling lots of balls right now. But I'm committed to self-care because the boys will need me to be available." She went on to say that as Brian's lung cancer diminished him physically she saw more clearly the living essence of her husband, as they depended on touch rather than words to express their love.

In the end, Brian died exactly as he prayed he would, with his wife and sons at his bedside and his extended family ranging around them. He was not in pain. He took his last breath quietly. He slipped away peacefully and went home.

35

Homeless to Homecoming

In the hushed hours of late evening just before Christmas, I was called to a nursing home in a northern suburb after the death of one of its residents. Family had been notified. It was almost midnight when I got there. A young woman in her early thirties was sitting quietly at the bedside. She introduced herself as Karen, the daughter of the deceased man whose body lay before us. Since I usually offer an anointing to honor the body and bless the spirit, I asked her if any other family members were on their way. She said no, and then asked, "Do you have time to hear our family story?"

I sat down in the subdued light of that still room. Then Karen proceeded to tell the tale of a man who had been orphaned early in his life and bounced from place to place, deprived of security and starved of love. Already an alcoholic before he grew up, he married young and became little else but an abusive presence in the lives of his wife and four children. Witnesses to his beatings of their mother and victims of his violent temper themselves, his children learned to fear and hate him. The day he abandoned them and disappeared from their lives was a "good riddance" day for them all. For years they knew nothing of him. But his sad legacy lived on in the family: Karen's brothers had problems with drugs and alcohol, and her sister married an alcoholic.

Their mother was permanently embittered by the years wasted on her husband.

Karen went on to say that six months earlier, her aunt had contacted her with news of her father. After many years of silence, he had finally called his sister. Having cycled through several jobs and several towns over the years, he was now both sick and homeless. His sister was afraid to take him in but told Karen of his plight and where she might be able to find him. Karen didn't hesitate. She drove several hours to the town he was living in, and, with persistent inquiry, she located him. Seeing his devastated condition, she had him hospitalized where he could be treated and safely go through detox. When it was determined that he was too sick to benefit from anything but hospice, Karen arranged for him to be transferred to a nursing home near where she lived and where he could receive our hospice care. She began to visit him daily. By this time, she had informed the rest of his family of his condition and whereabouts. They couldn't fathom her interest in becoming involved in his life and viewed it as a betrayal of their common experience of his violent history with them. Some of them had even stopped speaking to her because of it.

Early in her visits with her father, Karen realized that her hope of having some of the past healed by an expression of remorse from him had to be abandoned. By his studied avoidance of the past, she could tell that he so feared she would introduce it that he kept himself constantly guarded against her. She knew her father had few tools with which to deal with his past and little self-awareness of the harm he had caused. She realized that all they had was whatever they could make of the present in his newfound sobriety. She stated, "I decided to let go of the past and relate to my father solely in the present."

I asked her, "What made you choose differently from the rest of your family?" She replied, "I was five when he left, so I think I probably benefited from fewer years exposure to his abusive behavior, but there was something else too." She paused and then added hesitantly, "Even when he was being horrible to us, I never doubted I was loved—not by him, because he didn't know how to love—but by someone else. I didn't know who. But the feeling persisted that *somebody loves me.*

"One day I was walking home from school and saw a new sign outside a house that used to be boarded up. It advertised a church community that was moving into the neighborhood, and there was an invitation to children to come to Sunday school. So the following Sunday, I snuck out of my house without telling anyone where I was going and walked to this house church. That day in Sunday school we learned a song. It was 'Jesus Loves Me.' As I sang, I was suddenly struck with recognition. I thought to myself, *That's who loves me—it's Jesus*! I went home that day basking in my new discovery. I couldn't wait to go back the next Sunday.

"When Sunday finally came, I walked to the house only to find that it had been boarded up again and the sign taken down. It never reopened. But all year I held on to my discovery. Eventually, I found another church and went to it by myself. My family found out where I was going and laughed at me, but I didn't care. And as I grew up in this community, I discovered that God's love is real, and that I had found a new home. And since then, I have married and been blessed with a loving husband and two wonderful children."

She then recounted how, after a few visits with her father, she decided to tell her two young children that they had a grandfather who needed their love. On her next visit she brought them along and matter-of-factly introduced them, saying, "These are your grandchildren. They want to know you." Whereupon, the kids climbed up on his bed and shared some of their favorite picture books with him and made colored drawings that they pinned to his wallboard before leaving. "How did he react to this?" I asked. "Oh, he didn't know how to react at all," she said, laughing. "But we just kept coming back."

Karen added that as her father began to relax with his daughter, he began to look forward to visits with his grandchildren. By November, his health had stabilized enough to permit a pass to leave the nursing home and spend Thanksgiving Day with Karen and her family in their home. Pictures were taken that day and a small family photo album presented to him on their next visit. As he paged through it, Karen said, "You have a family now." He nodded wordlessly and carefully placed it on the table by his pillow. As Christmas drew near, he began to decline, and it became clear to Karen that her father would be leaving them soon. Karen's family brought an early Christmas to him at the nursing home.

Having finished her story, Karen handed me the photo album. The last photo showed a wasted man sitting up in bed, beaming—his arms around two young grandchildren who were nestled on either side of him. Karen commented, "At first I thought I might get a father back. I didn't. He couldn't give me that. But my children got a grandfather. That's *my* healing." We placed the album on his breast, open to that picture, and together, gave him a sending blessing.

I arrived home in the early hours of the morning, slipped quietly into bed, and thought, *What a gift it is to be a witness to these stories of love and loss and deep healing*. Lying in the dark, I took a moment to give thanks for the power of a forgiving heart and a homeless man's homecoming. Then I turned my gaze to my peacefully sleeping partner and gave thanks for my own homecoming.

THE LIGHT NEVER LEAVES US

It is the same light that graces the dawn,
blazes at noon, and bows to the evening shadows.

Daily our world is enlivened
by its face-to-face encounter
with the sun's warmth and brilliance.

Nightly our world turns away,
kindling the light as a memory and a promise.
Yet, we never forfeit the covenant of light
to accompany and preserve us.

The moon and stars woo our dreams
and the cold is held at bay.
In truth, the light never leaves us—
even in the darkest night.

~ Phyllis Zillhart [47]

Afterword

Since finishing this book, the Coronavirus (COVID-19) has suddenly become a global pandemic. Many businesses, restaurants, and libraries have closed their doors, and centers of worship have discontinued services. My family and I are in seclusion at home following orders to "shelter in place" issued by the Centers for Disease Control. Here in Minnesota, there is still some hope of containment, even as the statistics of those who have succumbed to the virus rise daily. I find myself having flashbacks to the pandemic of AIDS and all the young lives taken from us. But this time, we are all in it together.

At seventy-two, I am wary of suffering, but I am no longer afraid of death. The rainbow arc of my years has stretched beyond anything I could have imagined for myself. Despite challenges, I have been richly blessed. These days, my thoughts and prayers rest with my three-year-old grandson who shares our household, together with his parents. And with my beloved partner, Phyllis, who, as a hospice chaplain, stands on the front lines with those who are facing death in facilities beset by the virus. I pray daily for the steadfast workers and medical personnel who risk their lives and sacrifice time with their families in order to treat and care for patients who are strangers to them.

The community chorale I have been singing in has gone silent with the cancellation of what would have been our spring concert. But I am still practicing our music in the hope of returning to concertizing someday. Thankfully, it's hard to feel despondent while singing John Rutter's *Magnificat*. Meanwhile, our neighborhood watch association has invited households to come out of their seclusion each evening at seven, stand on their steps, and sing "Imagine" by John Lennon. Some of us are going around to nursing homes to sing outside the windows of lonely elders confined within. Between wearing a mask and practicing social distancing, there is a lot of space for love.

I don't know what lies ahead for my family or your family or for our world family. However, it is clear there has been and will be a significant measure of death and sorrow. In the midst of it all, we dare to trust that we are not alone. We are living at a time when we are all being called to claim home in relationship, sometimes remotely, other times musically, and always in blessing. We cannot allow fear to wall us up or tear us apart. I close with a prayer dear to my heart from the *Lutheran Book of Worship*:

"O God, support us all the day long of this troubled life, until the shadows lengthen and the evening comes and the busy world is hushed, the fever of life is over, and our work is done. Then, in your mercy, grant us a safe lodging and a holy rest, and peace at the last."

To my readers: If you found my book useful, please leave an honest review on the site through which you completed your purchase. Thank you for taking this journey with me in the sharing of this book, and for being among the many who continue to walk each other home.

Notes

Preface: THE SEARCH FOR HOME

1. Ram Dass, *How Can I Help: Stories and Reflections on Service,* coauthored by Ram Dass and Paul Gorman, Alfred A. Knopf, Inc., 1985.

PART ONE: COMING HOME TO OURSELVES

Chapter One: Welcome, Refuge, and Belonging

2. Anne-Sophie Mutter, from a Qobuz video interview, published April 14, 2014.

3. Cornel West, https://www.goodreads.com/quotes/279991-never-forget-that-justice-is-what-love-looks-like-in-public.

Chapter Two: Coming Home to Myself

4. C. S. Lewis, *The Last Battle, The Chronicles of Narnia,* Vol. 7, copyright 1956, HarperCollins.

PART TWO: FINDING HOME WITHIN COMMUNITY

Chapter Five: Celebration and Prosecution

5. Mari Irvin, the *St. Francis Cookbook,* now out of print.

6. "Conversion Therapy and LGBT Youth," Christy Mallory, Taylor N.T. Brown, and Kerith J. Conron, The Williams Institute, UCLA School of Law, January 2018.

Chapter Six: Hospitality in the Era of AIDS

7. Gina Kolata, "AIDS in San Francisco Hit Peak in '92," February 16, 1994, digitized version of an article from the *New York Times* print archive.

8. Appears to be a paraphrase from Thornton Wilder, *The Bridge of San Luis Rey.* Original passage: "There is a land of the living and a land of the dead and the bridge is love, the only survival, the only meaning" (p. 107). Top Ten Quotes, Novelguide.com, 1999.

9. "Diagnoses of HIV Infection in the United States and Dependent Areas," 2016 HIV Surveillance Report, Volume 28.

Chapter Eight: Family Ties within Community

10. Elizabeth Barrett Browning, poem, "To Flush, My Dog."

Chapter Eleven: Wedding Bells and Other Miracles

11. Melanie Mason, reporter for the *Los Angeles Times*, May 15, 2018. Information gathered from her article, "When Gavin Newsom issued marriage licenses in San Francisco, his party was furious. Now, it's a campaign ad."

12. "Same-Sex Marriage in California," World Heritage Encyclopedia, 2017.

PART THREE: MAKING LIVING SPACES LOVING PLACES

Chapter Seventeen: Overcoming Clutter with Sacred Giving

13. Mindfulness quote comes from the website of PsychologyToday.com.

14. Joseph Bruchac, "Sacred Giving, Sacred Receiving," *Parabola* Magazine, June 20, 2016.

Chapter Nineteen: Homes Occupied by Work and Electronics

15. Maya Angelou, in an interview with Oprah on the Oprah Winfrey Network (OWN).

16. Guy Johnson, in an interview with Oprah Winfrey on OWN, reports that from time to time, people would ask him what it was like to grow up in the shadow of his famous mother. His response to this was, "I didn't grow up in her shadow. I grew up in her light."

PART FOUR: FORMING AND SUPPORTING FAMILIES

17. The author encountered this quote years ago on a greeting card that attributed it to the American Home Economics Association, which in 1994 became known as the American Association of Family and Consumer Sciences. The author has been unable to corroborate the attribution with the current organization.

18. Jane Temple Howard, *Families,* 1978, ISBN 0-7658-0468-9.

Chapter Twenty-Four: Protecting Intimacy in Partnerships

19. Francis Bacon, AZquotes.com, Wind and Fly LTD, 2019, https://www.azquotes.com/quote/376449, accessed June 11, 2019.

20. Dag Hammarskjold, *Markings,* https://www.azquotes.com/author/6178-Dag_Hammarskjold.

Chapter Twenty-Six: Tipping Points for Change

21. The Library of Congress Web Guides: Primary Documents in American History, "The Indian Removal Act of 1830."

22. Cherokee Historical Association, "What Is the Trail of Tears?" www.cherokeemuseum.org/.

23. David Blight, from his course at Yale entitled "The Civil War and Reconstruction Era"; quoted in Ta-Nehisi Coates, "Slavery Made America," June 24, 2014.

24. The title of Ta-Nehisi Coates's article referenced in note 23.

25. Francis Scott Key, composer of the lyrics to the US National Anthem. After having watched the bombardment of Baltimore's Fort McHenry by the British Royal Navy on September 13, 1814, Key celebrated the American victory with a poem. The poem was adopted as the lyrics for the national anthem in 1931 by executive order from President Woodrow Wilson. The irony of the line "the land of the free" is that Key was a slaveholder who, as a US attorney, argued several cases against the abolitionist movement. "Francis Scott Key Pens 'The Star-Spangled Banner,'" History.com Editors, This Day in History, updated September 11, 2020, A&E Television Networks, Publisher.

26. "Social Justice Brief, Gun Violence in the American Culture," National Association of Social Workers.

27. ibid.

28. Terry Spencer of the Associated Press, "Stoneman Douglas Students Resolute as They Reenter Shooting Site," February 26, 2018.

29. Jennifer Calfas, "The Santa Fe High School Shooting in Texas Was the 22nd School Shooting This Year," Time.com, May 18, 2018.

30. "10 Years. 180 School Shootings. 356 Victims," CNN.com, July 2019.

Chapter Twenty-Seven: Families Seeking Refuge

31. Lisa Desjardins, Joshua Barajas, and Daniel Bush, "My son is not the same: New testimony paints bleak picture of family separation," *PBS NewsHour*, updated July 6, 2018.

32. Attorney General Jeff Sessions, June 20, 2018, immigration ruling. "While

migrant families seek shelter from violence, Trump administration narrows path to asylum," Emma Platoff, Alexa Ura, Jolie McCullough, and Darla Cameron, *Texas Tribune,* July 10, 2018.

33. AMMPARO: The Evangelical Lutheran Church in America's strategy to accompany migrant minors with protection, advocacy, representation, and opportunities. Envisioned for children and families forced to flee violence, poverty, environmental displacement, and lack of opportunities in their home communities. The Guardian Angels program is part of this initiative. Welcoming ELCA congregations partner children and families through their transition to life in the US. The word *amparo* in Spanish means the protection of a living creature from suffering or damage. www.elca.org/ammparo.

34. Minneapolis *Star Tribune* editorial, July 8, 2018, quote from Zaynab Abdi, immigrant from Yemen.

35. Sanctuary action taken in Milwaukee, August 8, 2019, https://www.prnewswire.com/news-releases/evangelical-lutheran-church-declares-itself-a-sanctuary-denomination-300898851.html. By vote of the 2019 ELCA Churchwide Assembly, the ELCA became America's first "sanctuary church body."

PART FIVE: GOING HOME: STORIES FROM HOSPICE

Chapter Twenty-Nine: Held in Blessing from Birth to Death

36. This quote is commonly attributed to Pierre Teilhard de Chardin but has also been attributed to G. I. Gurdjieff. Both are without sources. Attribution inconclusive.

37. The meaning of the Hebrew word *adam* is "earth creature," which derives from the stuff of which the "earth creature" is made, namely *adamah* or "earth." Bible Odyssey: "Adam/Adamah" by Samuel Thomas, associate professor, California Lutheran University.

38. The meaning of the Hebrew word *chavah,* which means "mother of all life," is loosely translated into English as "life." In the Talmud, Eve was called Chava because she "nursed the whole world" (Avodah Zarah 43a). "Eve's Name," Ask the Rabbi, aish.com.

39. The Hebrew word *ruah* or *ruach* means "breath" or "wind" and denotes God's presence.

40. This is similar to Christian Scripture, where the word for spirit in Greek is *pneuma,* which means "enlivening breath" or "wind."

41. "Hello" derives from *hail,* which was a shout of greeting or acclamation; derivations of it in Spanish, German, and Classical Greek add the meanings "health," "whole," or "be well." Hail was supplanted by the more contemporary word "hello," first recorded in the early 1800s (Merriam-Webster Word History).

Author's comments: In Christian Scripture, "hail" is a greeting of joy and peace. In the Gospel of Matthew 28:1-10, Jesus is depicted as making a resurrection appearance to the disciples after his execution. As he appears to them, Jesus first greets the stunned disciples with, "Hail."

42. "Goodbye" comes from late-sixteenth-century Old English as the blessing *godbwye,* which is a contraction of "God be with ye." "Good" became a later substitute for "God." English Language & Usage: "What is the origin of the word goodbye?" Online Etymology Dictionary, Douglas Harper, 2010.

Chapter Thirty-Two: Cultivating a Vibrant Spiritual Life

43. A saying commonly associated with Mother Teresa but whose attribution is undetermined.

44. Slogan on a campaign poster of Lori Swanson, attorney general of Minnesota.

45. Anne Lamott, *Traveling Mercies,* 1999, published in US by Pantheon Books, a division of Random House Inc., ISBN 0-679-44240-5.

46. Blessing offered to the people of St. Francis Lutheran Church by Rev. Phyllis Zillhart in 1990. The church adopted it for ongoing use in the liturgy for Holy Communion.

Chapter Thirty-Five: Homeless to Homecoming

47. A portion of the poem "The Light Never Leaves Us," by Phyllis Zillhart, carved into a granite slab in the Garden Memorial Terrace of St. Francis Lutheran Church, San Francisco.

Acknowledgments

Writing this book has not been a solitary exercise. I have received support from friends and family members who have previewed it in draft form and cheered my progress and its publication. I am deeply grateful to those whose stories and interviews have so enriched this book. I would like to specifically thank the following:

Phyllis Zillhart, my beloved spouse, for her unwavering love and support and her staunch belief that this book can help us all find our way home.

Noelle Hart, who has enriched our lives by her presence in our story, by the gift of our grandson, and by her commitment to justice in the world.

Evan Reynolds, who loves to adventure with his son, cook with his partner, and share with all of us his passion for tattoo artistry and graffiti art.

My grandson, Ciel, who helped me write this book by taking daily naps and whose presence reminds me to invest in the future every child deserves.

Jay Beatty and Charles Hinger, who provided free same-day delivery service and bravely teamed with us in parenthood.

Naomi Frost, for her generous support and for "being there" in all my important life moments.

Jan Drantell Johnson, for her endorsement and guidance in the writing of this book.

Kris Linner, for her endorsement, and *Evie Linner*, for her enthusiasm and hospitality.

Phoebe Worthington, for her generosity and belief in this book from its inception.

James Kowalski and Bruce Jervis, for their generosity and help in launching this book.

Jeff Johnson, who was once ordained with "a pair of lesbians" who made history with him, thanks to our extraordinary ordinations and his equally extraordinary gifts.

St. Francis Lutheran Church, the visionary village that helped raise our child, provided refuge and hope to countless people, and whose generosity helped bring this book to fruition.

James DeLange, for his prophetic leadership during our years together at St. Francis.

Our loved ones who have "crossed over" and whose stories live on in this world, blessing us as we seek to fully live the richness of our own story.

The dedicated and talented women of She Writes Press, whose hard work and expertise have graced this book and made it better.

My readers, who, through the purchase of this book, enable 50 percent of its royalties after publishing expenses to be given in support of people struggling to find home.

Recipients:

Crescent Cove Respite & Hospice Home for Kids: Cresecent Cove offers family-focused respite care and end-of-life care to children. A non-profit organization in Minnesota, it is the Midwest's first and only residential home-away-from-home for kids.

Kids in Need of Defense (KIND): A national nonprofit that protects unaccompanied children who enter the US immigration system. Their goal is to ensure that each child has pro bono legal representation that prioritizes the child's best interests, safety, and well-being.

About the Author

Sarah Pierce Photography/Minneapolis Headshots

RUTH FROST inspires people to create homes that tell their stories. A stained glass artisan, she designs custom windows for residences and churches. However, her other work in ministry and public advocacy taught her beauty alone cannot make a home. While living in San Francisco during the twin epidemics of AIDS and homelessness, Ruth worked closely with people profoundly disenfranchised from both home and family. Her spiritual community became a refuge of safety, hospitality, and belonging, key characteristics of home. Before leaving San Francisco in 2005, Ruth completed a 150-square-foot stained glass installation for a church in Sacramento depicting the Beloved Community of God in all its rainbow diversity.

Returning to Minneapolis, Ruth settled into the quieter side of soul-care, accompanying people on hospice care as they prepared to leave home to "go home." A trained legacy guide, Ruth helped people record their life stories and celebrate their legacies of love. She states, "My patients were my teachers. By their grace and courage in dying, they taught me how to live." Now retired, Ruth enjoys time with her family as well as writing, reading, and leading workshops and retreats on creating "Homes with Heart" and "Families of the Heart."

To contact Ruth, visit her website at www.ruthfrostwriter.com.

Reading Group Guide

A Welcome from the Author

Thank you for choosing *Homes with Heart* for your reading group. The chapters and questions offered for discussion are intended to spark discussion that can be as specific or as wide-ranging as the group wishes. Feel free to include other chapters that you found meaningful. Your questions are of equal importance to those in this guide.

Preface: THE SEARCH FOR HOME

"All we are doing is walking each other home."

1. Discuss what this quote means to you. How have you participated in walking someone home or been guided by someone who was/is doing that with you?

PART ONE: COMING HOME TO OURSELVES

Chapter One: Welcome, Refuge, and Belonging

"I believe the heart of every house is its hearth . . . whatever draws family and friends together."

2. Identify the hearth/heart of your home. How does it enliven you and those who enjoy your hospitality?

Chapter Two: Coming Home to Myself

Two pivotal moments helped the author "come home to herself." The first was the Pride Parade, and the second was "coming out" to her family.

3. How was each important?

Chapter Four: Leaving Home to Follow a Dream

The author has a strange experience going back to visit her family home. Years later, the author gets another chance to see it before its demolition. How was this healing? Share your experiences of revisiting home.

4. How do you carry home within you or find home in yourself?

PART TWO: FINDING HOME WITHIN COMMUNITY

Chapter Five: Celebration and Prosecution

Before the author testified at the hearing, a woman gave her a chip from the Berlin Wall. The author says she and Phyllis and Jeff *"carried the burden of giving voice to all those who were hostage to silent closets of fear and shame."* How did that gift help?

5. When have you realized that your words or actions reached beyond the scope of your individual life and made a difference greater than you anticipated?

While paddling their canoe at their lake refuge in Northern Minnesota, the author and her partner receive an unanticipated blessing.

6. How did this blessing connect to their current situation and to the blessing given to them earlier by the author's father? Discuss instances when you have heard the right words at the right time in your life.

Chapter Six: Hospitality in the Era of AIDS

The church community reached out to care for people with AIDS and their families.

7. How was the community a refuge for healing in the midst of so much death?

Chapter Seven: Getting to Know Our Homeless Neighbors

This chapter focuses on James, a mentally ill homeless man, and Victor, an affluent man with AIDS.

8. What do the two men have in common?

9. How could our lives and relationships change if we all shared the belief that "*in God's eyes, James deeply mattered, and so he was one of us.*"

Chapter Nine: Two Moms, Two Dads, and One Baby

Upon the birth of their child, the author describes receiving a message of welcome "redelivered" to her from her father. It taught her, "*Love has traveling power. Its messages are not bound by space or time.*"

10. How do you experience love's "traveling power"?

The author's family challenged societal norms and even its laws. Despite this, disparate people can sometimes bridge their differences with respect.

11. What was important about the encounter with the Chinese immigrant?

How do you think it affected those who witnessed it?

Chapter Ten: Embracing Transitions Together

This account shows how a family repeatedly transforms itself as new understandings inform old self-perceptions, reshaping individual and familial identities.

12. How do you think the ritual benefited Joshua and those present?

13. Discuss how societal and religious oppression interfere with self-identity. What does it take to become an authentic human being?

Chapter Eleven: Wedding Bells and Other Miracles

In 2004, the city of San Francisco began issuing marriage licenses to same-sex couples. Months later, these marriages were declared void by the California Supreme Court. Nonetheless, the author states, *"The joy of that day remains indelible in memory."*

14. Despite the disappointment that followed, why do you think the joy of that day was so resilient? What remains a source of strength in your life memories?

PART THREE: MAKING LIVING SPACES LOVING PLACES

Chapter Twelve: Homing with Children

"In our family, autonomy, creativity, and safety were important issues in parenting. We tried to practice love and boundaries, coupled with the acknowledgment that parents make mistakes just as their children do." Although they had agreed that the use of physical force was not "discipline," the author acknowledges spanking their child in an effort to curtail unsafe behavior. Her child's response showed her how ineffective and potentially harmful this was. The incident provided the catalyst for a different approach without physical force by means of nonviolent, age-appropriate consequences coupled with the possibility of making amends.

15. Reflect on some of the challenges of parenting you have experienced either from your parents' generation or in parenting your own children: How have you evolved?

The author says her daughter *"looks back on her childhood as having instilled in her a resilient spirit, a commitment to justice, and a high comfort level with difference. She rarely misses an opportunity to stand up and speak out."*

16. Give examples from your life of what can happen when children are invited to participate in efforts to make the world a better home for everyone.

Chapter Sixteen: Healing Painful Associations with Home

This story shows how ritual, together with supportive community, may initiate the process of healing following a traumatic event in the home. It also acknowledges the special bond people have with animals whose protective instincts help their humans.

17. As you imagine being among the group gathered for this ritual, what is its power? How do the recipient and the group benefit from it?

Chapter Seventeen: Overcoming Clutter with Sacred Giving

"Acquisitions obtained impulsively end up cluttering our home environments, fraying family relationships, and wreaking havoc with family budgets . . . they mask our true yearnings. Acquisition becomes the false solution for lives that are out of balance."

18. What are some of the "true yearnings" that may be obscured by a life that is "out of balance"?

The good news is that we can challenge our own beliefs about ourselves . . . internalized by shame. By changing patterns of thinking, we can change the way we feel and act.

19. What are some ways we can promote positive changes in our thinking that ground us in purposeful living?

Discuss the approach to clutter Marie Kondo takes in determining what "sparks joy." Consider how the ritual of the "giveaway" promotes gratitude in community.

Chapter Eighteen: Using Symbols to Hold Memories

"When we have difficulty letting go of things, symbols have the power to represent . . . what we think we could lose. They . . . connect us with those who have gone before us."

20. How do symbols function in your life? Share one important to you.

Chapter Twenty: Creating Decor That Tells Your Story

Meaningful decor is what you create when you surround yourself with things that inspire, move, or uplift you and help you remember people and events precious to you.

21. In your home, how does your decor represent people, events, and stories you want to remember?

PART FOUR: FORMING AND SUPPORTING FAMILIES

Chapter Twenty-One: Choosing Families of the Heart

This chapter shows how to cultivate "families of the heart" to enhance quality of life and help heal old wounds that have framed our experiences early in life. Discuss how the following questions illumine your relationships:

22. "Is this a life-giving relationship that calls out and affirms the best in me?"

"Do I like who I am with this person?"

23. "Am I accepted without judgment when I show my vulnerabilities?"
"Do my friends care about working for a kinder and more just society?"

Chapter Twenty-Seven: Families Seeking Refuge

In asking the question *"What does home mean to you?"* the author says the responses she most frequently gets are: *"a place of refuge where it's safe to be myself"* and *"a place I share with people I love."* This chapter reflects on the global crisis of homelessness as people flee violence and economic insecurity. It raises concerns about the direction the US is charting and its practices with respect to new arrivals, especially families and unaccompanied children from Central America who cross our southern border.

Discuss this dream of the Muslim immigrant from Yemen:

"I dream of a world where there is no war or violence, a world where there is peace and love. I dream of a world where newcomers are not seen as aliens or illegals, where we all see and celebrate our shared humanity, and families are able to live together."

Consider the following invitation:

"Let us all make America gracious again, and in the process, become citizens of the world. Let us make home—that place of safety, hospitality, and belonging—a universal human right!"

24. What is our collective responsibility to this dream and this invitation?

Chapter Twenty-Eight: Opening Home and Heart

Discuss how the couple in this interview opened their home and welcomed an immigrant woman and her baby into their lives and hearts.

25. How were all their lives changed as a result? Discuss a time when you made a difference to someone by your welcome or someone did that for you.

PART FIVE: GOING HOME: STORIES FROM HOSPICE

Chapter Twenty-Nine: Held in Blessing from Birth to Death

In this chapter the author reflects on spirituality and what it means to be human. She says, *I have come to believe that we humans do not have souls —we are souls . . . we all seek to make a home here because the longing for home is innate."* She is convinced that we all share divine breath and a common purpose: to love one another, to tend life, and to preserve space for all to thrive.

26. What difference could it make to see oneself (and others) as "being" a soul versus "having" a soul—with a longing for home that is innate?
Through the power of love, we are supported in our coming and our going by

these two blessings: the one given to the newborn, "Hello, little one, be well and truly welcome," and that given to the dying one, "Goodbye, dear one, God be with you, travel well."

27. Discuss the meaning of "hello" and "goodbye."

What happens when you view your life as being held by, and sustained between, these two blessings? Why is it important to bless one another?

Chapter Thirty: Lessons in Living from the Dying

After her mother's death, the author finds a list in her mother's hymnal of gifts given and gifts received.

28. Discuss her mother's prescription for living a good life.

"Thanks to my work in hospice, I know that none of my loved ones who have passed on are lost to me. I believe our loved ones know and love us and send us their blessings from the vantage point of their best selves and their deepest healing . . . none of us need be stuck in our worst moments of this life . . . we don't need to keep living them because our loved ones certainly aren't. We are loved and forgiven unconditionally right here in this moment. And forever hereafter."

29. If you could trust this is true, how would it affect the way you live your life?

Chapter Thirty-Two: Cultivating a Vibrant Spiritual Life

Spirituality is grace, gratitude, and gift. It is both personal and communal. There are no insiders and no outsiders, no chosen and no un-chosen. We are all one . . . when a religion loses spirituality, it has lost its heart, and terrible things are then said and done in the name of that religion and its corrupted deity.

30. What do you think the author means by saying you can be spiritual without being religious, but you can't be religious without being spiritual? Do you agree? Why or why not?

In our elder years, the most important gift we have is the gift we have become, because of how we have lived and how we have been loved. Our legacy is love; the gift is grace.

31. As you consider the author's keys to finding a vibrant spiritual life, which do you especially resonate with? What would you add?

The author ends this section of the book with the following statement:

Home is ultimately a spiritual journey, in good company. The way home is love. Our destination is our beginning, the Lover of us all.

32. What is the essence of your learning regarding home?

In Conclusion

Choose your favorite story from the last three chapters and discuss it with others who chose it. Reassemble and share highlights of your discussion with the large group.

SELECTED TITLES FROM SHE WRITES PRESS

She Writes Press is an independent publishing company founded to serve women writers everywhere. Visit us at www.shewritespress.com.

Falling Together: How to Find Balance, Joy, and Meaningful Change When Your Life Seems to be Falling Apart by Donna Cardillo. $16.95, 978-1-63152-077-8. A funny, big-hearted self-help memoir that tackles divorce, caregiving, burnout, major illness, fears, and low self-esteem—and explores the renewal that comes when we are able to meet these challenges with courage.

Renewable: One Woman's Search for Simplicity, Faithfulness, and Hope by Eileen Flanagan. $16.95, 978-1-63152-968-9. At age forty-nine, Eileen Flanagan had an aching feeling that she wasn't living up to her youthful ideals or potential, so she started trying to change the world—and in doing so, she found the courage to change her life.

Filling Her Shoes: Memoir of an Inherited Family by Betsy Graziani Fasbinder. $16.95, 978-1-63152-198-0. A "sweet-bitter" story of how, with tenderness as their guide, a family formed in the wake of loss and learned that joy and grief can be entwined cohabitants in our lives.

Fire Season: A Memoir by Hollye Dexter. $16.95, 978-1-63152-974-0. After she loses everything in a fire, Hollye Dexter's life spirals downward and she begins to unravel—but when she finds herself at the brink of losing her husband, she is forced to dig within herself for the strength to keep her family together.

Painting Life: My Creative Journey Through Trauma by Carol K. Walsh. $16.95, 978-1-63152-099-0. Carol Walsh was a psychotherapist working with traumatized clients when she encountered her own traumatic experience; this is the story of how she used creativity and artistic expression to heal, recreate her life, and ultimately thrive.

All Set for Black, Thanks: A New Look at Mourning by Miriam Weinstein. $16.95, 978-1-63152-109-6. A wry, irreverent take on how we mourn, how we remember, and how we keep our dead with us even as we (sort of) let them go.

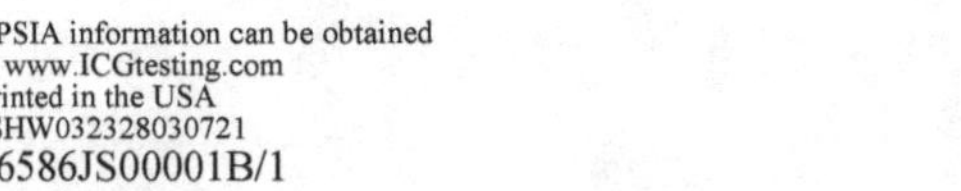

CPSIA information can be obtained
at www.ICGtesting.com
Printed in the USA
JSHW032328030721
16586JS00001B/1

9 781647 421182